CRJC
12/14

KIDS

WHO ARE

CHANGING

THE WORLD

Sourcebooks and the colophon are registered trademarks of Sourcebooks, Inc.

A book conceived and created by Olivier Blond, for GoodPlanet. The Good Planet Foundation's mission is to raise awareness about ecology and sustainable development.

Originally published as *Ces enfants qui changent le monde*, © Editions de La Martinière, 2012.

This publication is designed to provide accurate and authoritative information in regard to the subject matter covered. It is sold with the understanding that the publisher is not engaged in rendering legal, accounting, or other professional service. If legal advice or other expert assistance is required, the services of a competent professional person should be sought. —From a Declaration of Principles Jointly Adopted by a Committee of the American Bar Association and a Committee of Publishers and Associations

Published by Sourcebooks Jabberwocky, an imprint of Sourcebooks, Inc.
P.O. Box 4410, Naperville, Illinois 60567-4410
(630) 961-3900
Fax: (630) 961-2168
www.jabberwockykids.com

Originally published in 2012 in France by Editions de La Martinière, an imprint of La Martinière Groupe, Paris.

Library of Congress Cataloging-in-Publication data is on file with the publisher.

Source of Production: Leo Paper, Heshan City, Guangdong Province, China
Date of Production: August 2014
Run Number: 4500

Printed and bound in China.

LEO 10 9 8 7 6 5 4 3 2 1

KIDS WHO ARE CHANGING THE WORLD

A BOOK FROM THE GOODPLANET FOUNDATION

PHOTOGRAPHS BY YANN ARTHUS-BERTRAND

TEXT BY ANNE JANKÉLIOWITCH

sourcebooks
jabberwocky

KIDS ARE THE FUTURE

Old ideas about ecology that haven't been rethought and updated are partly responsible for the current ecological crisis. Young people creating new ideas or reinventing old ones is essential in changing the future global health of our planet. That's why my foundation, GoodPlanet, places so much importance on children's education. GoodPlanet builds schools in developing countries and distributes free educational materials to those schools. I want to thank the staff and students of the twelve French schools who wanted to name their school after me in order to recognize the educational importance of my work as a photographer and my commitment to the planet.

Young people are full of optimism and we all need that. They have not given up and they have not given in. They sometimes feel passionately about the terrible things adults are doing to the planet. They are concerned about what will happen to the future of Earth. They want to speak out like Severn Suzuki did over twenty years ago in her famous speech in Rio. She was only twelve at the time.

Kids have an amazing ability to come up with exciting ideas and carry them out with remarkable energy. When I first met Felix Finkbeiner, I struggled to believe that this boy, aged 14, led a group that had taken on a United Nations project. Felix had inspired people to plant trees throughout his country. Later, I had the opportunity to meet other young people who were involved with the United Nations Environment Programme (called Tunza). I was amazed to see these kids from all different countries come together and share the incredible enthusiasm they felt for saving our planet. They may be young, but they have something to teach us about commitment, perseverance, and sometimes even bravery. They show us that we must believe in ourselves and in our ability to change the world. The future is ours to shape; we hold it in our hands.

Together, these young people are changing the world and sending a message of hope. Though this book profiles forty kids working for the environment, there are thousands more from all over the world doing their part. Maybe you're one of them. Or perhaps this book will inspire you to *become* one of them.

Yann Arthus-Bertrand
President of the GoodPlanet Foundation

THE GIRL WHO SILENCED THE WORLD FOR SIX MINUTES

SEVERN CULLIS-SUZUKI,
12 YEARS OLD IN 1992, CANADA

BACKGROUND

In 2012, twenty years after the first Earth Summit in 1992, Rio de Janeiro once again hosted this international meeting of people working for the future of the planet.

I'm only a child and I don't have all the solutions, but I want you to realize, neither do you!

"You don't know how to fix the holes in our ozone layer. You don't know how to bring salmon back up a dead stream. You don't know how to bring back an animal now extinct. And you can't bring back forests that once grew where there is now desert. If you don't know how to fix it, please stop breaking it!"

It's not every day that a child gets the chance to look into the eyes of the world's leaders and speak to them about important issues. But that's what happened to Severn Cullis-Suzuki in 1992 when she was twelve years old. At the age of nine, she'd worked with a group of friends to found the ECO (Environmental Children's Organization), a group created to educate children about environmental issues. Each year her concern for the environment continued to grow. In 1992, Severn raised enough money to attend the Earth Summit in Rio de Janeiro.

The statue of Christ overlooking Guanabara Bay and Greater Rio de Janeiro. Rio de Janerio hosted the first Earth Summit in 1992.

"LOSING MY FUTURE IS NOT LIKE LOSING AN ELECTION OR A FEW POINTS ON THE STOCK MARKET. I AM HERE TO SPEAK FOR ALL GENERATIONS TO COME."

Only a few children attended the 1992 Earth Summit, and the schedule didn't have room for them to participate in the conference. Severn was in a session attended by delegates from all over the world. When one of the speakers dropped out, Severn was allowed to speak to the United Nations delegates.

SEVERN CULLIS-SUZUKI

"I CHALLENGE YOU; PLEASE MAKE YOUR ACTIONS REFLECT YOUR WORDS."

SEVERN CULLIS-SUZUKI

In a clear, calm voice, Severn stood at the podium and gave her speech. Severn's talk was directed at government officials, politicians, business leaders, and news reporters. "In my life, I have dreamed of seeing the great herds of wild animals, jungles and rain forests full of birds and butterflies, but now I wonder if they will even exist for my children to see."

"Did you have to worry about these little things when you were my age?" Her remarks were so sincere and honest that she had the complete attention of everyone listening to her. For a few minutes, the delegates could even imagine it was their own daughter speaking.

"At school, even in kindergarten, you teach us to behave in the world. You teach us not to fight with others, to work things out, to respect others, to clean up our mess, not to hurt other creatures, to share—not be greedy. Then why do you go out and do the things you tell us not to do?"

When Severn was finished speaking, the delegates applauded her. Many of them sat in their seats saying nothing, thinking about what she had said. That is why Severn is called "the girl who silenced the world for six minutes."

Severn wanted the listeners to realize that they weren't just attending the Earth Summit as delegates; many of them were parents and grandparents. "My father always says, 'You are what you do, not what you say.' Well, what you do makes me cry at night. You grown-ups say you love us. I challenge you; please make your actions reflect your words."

Twenty years later, the video of Severn's speech has become an Internet success. For Severn, if the clip continues to affect people, it is because young people want to express themselves. "I think it's still so popular because it speaks to the need for—and the power of—the voice of youth. Adults need to be reminded of the consequences of their actions, even though they have multiple interests and ulterior motives. Young people see things for what they are and call their elders on their actions. Youth doesn't know what isn't possible."

Has the challenge that Severn gave world leaders in her speech changed anything? Severn believes that people today know much more about the good things they can do for the environment. For example, in 1992 the disappearance of the ozone layer was a major environmental issue. Thanks to the Montreal Protocol treaty, which was activated in 1989, countries from around the world agreed to phase out the production of numerous substances believed to be bad for the ozone layer. It is believed that the ozone layer will recover by 2050.

Severn is now the mother of two young children. Since giving her famous speech, she has continued to act to preserve the planet. Severn has worked with environmental groups, written a book, hosted a television show, and attended many other world summit meetings. In 2012 she attended the 20th anniversary of the World Summit. Severn was happy to see that young people who represented more than half the world's population were included in the conference meetings and presentations.

PROTECTING THE ENVIRONMENT IS A LOGICAL MATTER!

CASSANDRA LIN, 10 YEARS OLD IN 2008, WESTERLY, RHODE ISLAND, UNITED STATES

BACKGROUND

To save fuel, oil can be recycled from fryers to heat homes and even run cars.

Because she had always been curious about what was going on around her, Cassandra noticed something strange in her city. First, there were poor families who didn't have enough money to keep warm during the winter. Second, there were sewage pipes that were clogged due to the oils and fats from kitchen sinks. She was also aware of a worldwide problem: the frequent use of oil disrupted the global climate by emitting greenhouse gases.

Cassandra discussed these issues with several of her friends. One day, while visiting an exhibition about the environment, she discovered that used cooking oil could be turned into biodiesel, a cleaner fuel than oil. That was the answer to the problems facing her city.

A doe in a field of rapeseed in the valley of Chevreuse, France. Rapeseed is the main source of biofuel in France.

"A COMPANY COLLECTS THE WASTE OIL TO TURN INTO BIODIESEL."

CASSANDRA LIN

Cassandra and her four friends convinced their mayor to install a new container to collect waste oils and fats. They raised awareness of their project by appearing on the radio and making presentations in schools. They spoke with shoppers leaving supermarkets about recycling their cooking oil, and also worked to convince the restaurants of the city to participate. A company became a partner of the project and collected the waste oil to bring to a factory where it could be turned into biodiesel. Part of the biodiesel was given to humanitarian organizations that distributed it free of charge to poor families who used it for heating their homes.

CASSANDRA LIN

8

OBJECTIVE:

Develop energy sources that don't contribute to global warming.

• •

ACTION: Collect edible oils and recycle them into biodiesel.

HOW I'VE CHANGED THE WORLD: Over 50,000 gallons of oil are collected and recycled into biodiesel annually. And every winter, 50 poor families' homes are heated with free biodiesel.

WHAT MAKES ME THE HAPPIEST: My project is useful for both the environment and the people of my city.

WHAT ROLE DID MY PARENTS PLAY: They have always guided, helped, and encouraged me to be curious about everything!

MY ADVICE: Don't aim too high! For example, start by volunteering somewhere, helping at an animal shelter or sorting recycling. Then move forward by setting goals that you are able to achieve.

WHAT I DO NOW: I'm working to extend the project to other cities in the region.

MY MOST HEROIC ACTION: Changing the law! We managed to pass a new law that requires businesses that use or sell cooking oil to recycle it.

MY BIGGEST MISTAKE: With the restaurants, at the beginning, the people in charge didn't have time to meet with us. So we changed our strategy: we'd call for an appointment and present the project in five minutes with a little video. It was much more effective. Today, we believe more than 100 restaurants in 12 cities are recycling their oil.

CASSANDRA LIN

9

GIVE NEW LIFE TO COMPUTERS— IT'S EASY!

ALEX LIN, 11 YEARS OLD IN 2005, WESTERLY, RHODE ISLAND, UNITED STATES

BACKGROUND
Electronic waste contains hazardous materials, which are harmful to the environment when they are thrown away.

In the Lin family, everyone works to do good things for the environment. "It's a way of life," says Alex. He discovered a newspaper article that said electronic waste pollutes the environment and accumulates in the millions. For Alex, tackling the problem of electronic waste was his challenge.

"At first, it felt like we were at the foot of a huge mountain. We didn't know where to start to try and deal with the problem," recalls Alex. But with a group of his friends, they set goals and began to move forward.

The first task was to get people to recycle. They got their city to install a special container for electronic waste. Then they found a recycling company that specialized in collecting electronic waste. Today, because of the waste container, old computers are no longer thrown in the landfill. That is progress!

A wasteland of electrical appliances in Aspropyrgos, Greece. In other countries, the law requires recycling of electronic and electrical waste. People are allowed to return an electronic item to the store that sold it to them.

"WE HAVE EQUIPPED SCHOOLS IN SRI LANKA, MEXICO, THE PHILIPPINES, AND KENYA WITH COMPUTER ROOMS AND ADDED AN INTERNET CAFÉ IN CAMEROON."

ALEX LIN

If you can, try to reuse rather than recycle. "Reusing something is seven times more effective than recycling," says Alex. Alex's friends tinker with old computers donated by businesses. "We change the hard drive, add memory and programs—it's easy." The refurbished computers get a second life when they are sent to places that need them. "We have equipped schools in Sri Lanka, Mexico, the Philippines, and Kenya with computer rooms and added an Internet café in Cameroon," says Alex.

Another good thing that happened was that the laws were changed. Since 2006, thanks to Alex and his friends, it is now mandatory to recycle electronic waste in the state of Rhode Island.

• •

ACTION: Recycle electronic waste and repackage old computers.

HOW I'VE CHANGED THE WORLD: 180 tons of electronic waste were recycled from 2005 to 2011. More than 350 refurbished computers were given to schools that needed them. 7 computer rooms are now equipped with refurbished computers in developing countries. Approximately 1 million people are now aware of the benefits of recycling electronic waste.

WHAT MAKES ME HAPPIEST: The school where we sent computers in Sri Lanka decided to call itself the WIN school, the name we gave our environmental group. It was really cool to see that our project had an impact across the world.

WHAT I'M MOST PROUD OF: This is causing a permanent change in my city and my state.

MY BIGGEST MISTAKE: The first waste recycling law that we proposed was too complicated. It was rejected. So we created a simpler version, and we talked about the project on the radio, in newspapers, and in schools. We got people to sign our petition, and in 2006, the law was passed.

MY ADVICE: Find something that excites you, and do it. If you're not passionate about something, it's harder to stay motivated when things get complicated.

WHAT I DO NOW: Work with other youth groups that are helping the environment so everyone can benefit from my experience.

ALEX LIN

Fisherman on the reservoir of the Imboulou Dam in the Republic of Congo. Dams are the main source of renewable energy in the world.

I WANT MY CHILDREN TO SEE LIVING CAMELS.

CAMERON OLIVER, 11 YEARS OLD IN 2008, LIVES IN THE UNITED ARAB EMIRATES, ABU DHABI

OBJECTIVE:
Save camels from the dangers of litter.

ACTION: Educate the public and pick up litter.

HOW I'VE CHANGED THE WORLD: Thousands of people are aware of the problem of litter left behind in nature.

WHAT I'M MOST PROUD OF: Out of 43,000 nominees, my campaign was awarded a prize from Abu Dhabi in 2008 for bettering the environment. I am the youngest person ever to receive it.

WHAT ROLE DID MY PARENTS PLAY: At the beginning of my project, they were my only supporters, and they provided the money to fund my efforts.

WHAT MY FRIENDS THINK: They support my campaign 100 percent!

MY ADVICE: My dad always says, "The small streams make big rivers." So no matter the size of your efforts, even small drops of water are helpful.

WHAT I DO NOW: I talk with store owners about litter disposal. I ask taxi drivers to put my bumper sticker on their cars. And I continue to visit schools and talk with the media about my campaign.

It all started with a newspaper article in which Cameron learned that two camels died from eating litter left behind by humans.

Cameron was shocked by this discovery and decided to make the public aware of the problem. "Camels are a part of this country. Men need them, and yet we kill them!" When Cameron was in sixth grade, he organized a display in his school explaining the dangers litter and trash pose to camels. Gradually, more and more people became aware of Cameron's campaign. Through the use of a website, stickers, baseball caps, pamphlets, posters, and television coverage, people learned about the consequences of littering.

Camel caravan near Nouakchott in Mauritania.

Cameron's next step was to organize his classmates and volunteers to remove litter and other deadly waste from the desert.

Cameron's goal remains clear. "As long as camels are dying, I will not stop my campaign. I want my children to see living camels."

www.cameronscamelcampaign.com

CAMERON OLIVER

MUSIC HELPS ME BRING THE WORLD'S CHILDREN TOGETHER.

AITAN GROSSMAN, 12 YEARS OLD IN 2009, PALO ALTO, CALIFORNIA, UNITED STATES

● ● ● ● ● ● ● ● ● ● ● ● ● ● ● ● ● ● ●

BACKGROUND
An Inconvenient Truth is a book and a documentary film that shows how and why the Earth's climate is affected by people.

When he finished reading the book *An Inconvenient Truth* by Al Gore, Aitan understood that global warming was a serious problem that would affect the lives of the next 100 generations. Aitan was concerned about the issue, but wondered what he could do to help.

Because he loved music, Aitan chose to do something through song. But to really educate children on all continents of the world, Aitan knew the song would have to be a universal one that everyone could sing in their own language. It had to be a song that could move beyond borders. Aitan sent his song to schools in all five continents searching for kids like him—kids who were concerned about global warming and wanted to send a loud and strong message. Classes from different countries responded to Aitan's call. In the original version of his song, Aitan sang with children from Botswana, France, Venezuela, Taiwan, Ethiopia, and the United States.

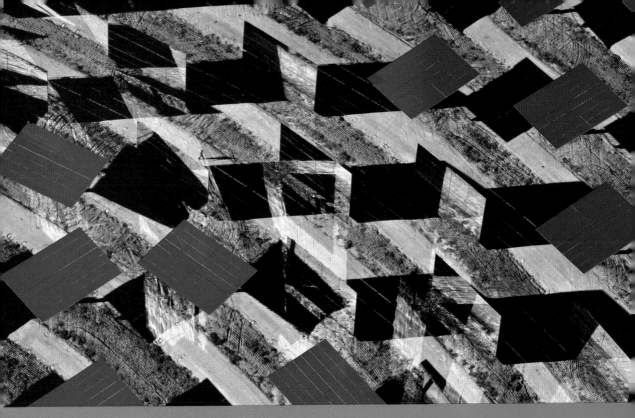

Mirrors of a solar power plant near Seville, Spain.

"IN THE ORIGINAL VERSION OF HIS SONG, AITAN SANG WITH CHILDREN FROM BOTSWANA, FRANCE, VENEZUELA, TAIWAN, ETHIOPIA, AND THE UNITED STATES."

AITAN GROSSMAN

KIDS WHO ARE CHANGING THE WORLD

FROM THE SONG
"100 GENERATIONS":

The air is getting warm,
My eyes are burning.
This is the biggest storm,
The tide is turning
I see the waving wheat,
I see the redwood tree,
They wither in the heat.
What will become of me?

Aitan created the KidEarth website, where you can download musical accompaniment and lyrics to the song. Any group of children in any country of the world is free to create their own version of "100 Generations." They can film themselves singing the song and then send the video to Aitan so he can post it on the website. At the KidEarth site you can also contribute by downloading the original version of "100 Generations" for less than one dollar. All the proceeds from the downloads go to organizations working against the threat of global warming.

www.kidearth.us

OBJECTIVE: Make children aware of the consequences of global warming.

ACTION: Compose a song.

HOW I'VE CHANGED THE WORLD:
I alerted thousands of children about the problem of global warming. The KidEarth website has received 700,000 visitors from 110 different countries.

WHAT MAKES ME THE HAPPIEST:
Hearing other children from around the world singing my song. Each time I tell myself, "This is cool. I don't know these people, but we want to spread the same message!"

WHAT I'M MOST PROUD OF:
Talking about my project at conferences. I gave a speech before the US Environmental Protection Agency about the environment. People always seemed to appreciate what I did.

MY BIGGEST MISTAKE: Selling the song as a download on the Internet didn't work very well at first. At one point I realized that awareness of the song and its message was more important than trying to raise money. When I made the song available for free, many more listeners learned about it and my project really took off.

MY ADVICE: Be creative and original. If you are innovative, people will listen.

WHAT ROLE DID MY PARENTS PLAY: I would never have succeeded if I hadn't had the support of my parents and my music teacher. My father helped with mixing the recording of the song. He also helped create the logo and website for KidEarth.

WHAT MY FRIENDS THINK: They recorded the song with me!

AITAN GROSSMAN

21

USING DISPOSABLE BOTTLES MAKES NO SENSE.

PARRYS RAINES, 16 YEARS OLD, AUSTRALIA

BACKGROUND

Much of our waste and litter ends up in the oceans. This is the case with plastic bottles that threaten fish, turtles, and dolphins.

Where did you get the idea to ban disposable plastic bottles at your school? I love to swim and surf in the ocean. So when I learned about the threat plastic pollution poses to marine life I decided to take action. I wanted to educate other kids about reducing their usage of disposable plastic bottles. Using a bottle once and throwing it away makes no sense.

What did you do? I wrote a letter about the project and presented it to the principal of my school. It had statistics about marine pollution caused by plastics, as well as a proposal to reduce the use of disposable bottles in our school.

And the principal accepted your proposal? Yes! The school has purchased about 1,000 reusable metal water bottles, and installed three water fountains for refilling the bottles. Students' families donated small amounts of money for buying the metal bottles. The day of the official start of the project, I gave a presentation to the whole school to explain the importance of what we were doing.

Bottle racks near Braunschweig, Germany. The amount of oil used in manufacturing, packaging, and transporting a water bottle is equivalent to one quarter of the water contained in the bottle.

"WHEN PEOPLE SEE US WALKING AROUND TOWN CARRYING OUR REUSABLE BOTTLES THEY KNOW WE'RE MAKING A STATEMENT ABOUT THE ENVIRONMENT."

PARRYS RAINES

What did the students think about your project? Most were surprised to learn how harmful plastics were to marine life. They quickly adopted using the new metal bottles.

Have other schools followed your example? I presented the results of my work to many schools in 2011, accompanied by a short film I'd made. Each time I spoke, people told me afterward that they were really excited. Even if a school doesn't adopt the program I think students will do it on their own.

"IN THE MIDDLE OF THE PACIFIC OCEAN IS AN ISLAND OF PLASTIC TRASH, KNOWN AS THE GREAT PACIFIC GARBAGE PATCH. EACH YEAR, HUNDREDS OF THOUSANDS OF MARINE LIFE ARE POISONED OR SUFFOCATED BY PLASTIC TRASH."

Reduce plastic litter in the oceans.

ACTION: Remove disposable plastic bottles used by students and replace them with reusable stainless steel water bottles.

HOW I'VE CHANGED THE WORLD: I opened the eyes of a lot of young people to the large quantities of plastic in the sea and the harm it does to marine life.

WHAT MAKES ME THE HAPPIEST: I like seeing all the students with their reusable water bottles at school. And when you walk around town, you see people using them there too. It sends an ecological message to people who see us using the bottles. In fact, parents have asked where they can buy reusable bottles for their whole family.

WHAT I AM MOST PROUD OF: I admire our principal because he had the courage to implement this action and to make our school a model for the whole area.

WHAT ROLE DID MY PARENTS PLAY: They really encourage me and help me to reach my goals.

MY ADVICE: Start with a small goal that you can communicate to your family and friends, and then to your school. Gather facts and figures to explain the problem, and then propose a solution.

WHAT I DO NOW: Continue to inform young people about environmental problems through my website www.climategirl.com.au/

PARRYS RAINES

MY ORGANIZATION, PLANT PATROL, STOPPED THE INVASION OF NON-NATIVE PLANTS.

ERIC BABB, 11 YEARS OLD IN 2007,
UTAH, UNITED STATES

• •

BACKGROUND

Plant seeds can sometimes travel very far, even from one continent to another. If they find good growing conditions, they start to multiply in a new area and become invasive.

Right page: Boats floating in a bed of water hyacinth on the Nile River in Egypt. This is an invasive species that multiplies very quickly, covering bodies of water and preventing other species from growing and developing.

Meeting invaders from another place isn't something found only in science fiction books. While hiking in a park, Eric noticed some plants growing alongside the trail that he didn't recognize. With the help of his sister, a naturalist, he learned the plants were Dalmatian toadflax, an invasive, nonnative plant that is toxic to local wildlife. Because of his love for nature and animals, Eric decided he had to go on the attack and try to get rid of the invasive plants. But there's only so much one person can do. It would take an army to remove all the Dalmatian Toadflax. That's when Eric decided to create Plant Patrol, a group that identifies and removes invasive plants.

Eric organizes volunteer training in schools at the annual county fair with scout trips and with regional religious groups. He explains the danger of nonnative plants and shows people how to remove them and prevent them from coming back. Additionally, Plant Patrol has a day where over 100 people gather together to plant native herbs and flowers in areas where invasive plants have been uprooted.

OBJECTIVE: Remove invasive plants.

ACTION: Uprooting and destroying invasive plants.

HOW I'VE CHANGED THE WORLD: More than 2,200 people in my community are now aware of the problem of invasive species. Together, we have spent 3,700 hours pulling up nonnative plants.

WHAT MAKES ME THE HAPPIEST: When I revisit areas where invasive plants have been uprooted, I see fewer of them growing there. That makes me feel like I've really changed things. Of course, my project doesn't have an impact on the whole world. But it's improved a corner of it.

WHAT I'M MOST PROUD OF: The number of people who now know that invasive plants are a threat to nature.

WHAT MY FRIENDS THINK: Many of my friends helped me by participating in Plant Patrol activities. Last year my class took a Plant Patrol field trip.

MY ADVICE: Just look around you. Is there something that's a local problem? If everyone took care of one small problem that was right next door, the whole world would be a better place.

WHAT I DO NOW: I've continued my campaign by creating a blog to inform the public about dangerous invasive plants. These plants are a major problem and they are everywhere.

ERIC BABB

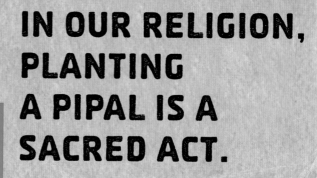

IN OUR RELIGION, PLANTING A PIPAL IS A SACRED ACT.

ANUP RAJ CHALISE,
15 YEARS OLD IN 2010, NEPAL

• •

BACKGROUND In the Hindu religion in Nepal, the pipals (or fig trees) are respected and revered. The trees provide a place of worship.

Where did you get the idea to plant sacred trees? Climate change is a major problem. Everyone should know what causes global warming, why it's a serious problem, and how to act to prevent it. But in Nepal, it isn't something people think about. Many Nepalese are poor and have little education. For them there are more immediate problems than climate change.

So how did you encourage them to act in a way that would help the problem of global warming? Instead of trying to use scientific explanations I talked to them in a language they understood: religious language. I suggested that we plant pipals, which are sacred trees.

Trees growing in Guyana. 300 species of trees can be found in a single acre of rain forest.

"DURING THEIR GROWTH, TREES ABSORB GASES. THIS HELPS MANAGE GLOBAL WARMING."

ANUP RAJ CHALISE

ANUP RAJ CHALISE

How did you go about setting up your campaign to plant pipals? I asked a local nature protection organization to help me start the campaign and help raise awareness. We were interviewed on the radio and the word started to spread among youth groups and schools about the value of trees. The first pipals were planted on Earth Day in 2010. It worked so well that other organizations were inspired by our project and began planting trees in other parts of Nepal!

www.ficusreligiosaanup.yolasite.com

OBJECTIVE: Plant Trees

ACTION: Organize a major campaign for planting pipals.

HOW I'VE CHANGED THE WORLD: 200 pipals were planted in 2010 and about 2,000 in 2011 by hundreds of volunteers.

MY BIGGEST MISTAKE: At first I wanted to set up the project all by myself, but I wasn't successful. People weren't interested because they thought I was too young. But when I reached out for help from the media, it generated attention for the project and people wanted to work with me. I learned the importance of teamwork.

MY ADVICE: Action speaks more than words.

WHAT MAKES ME THE HAPPIEST: It started as one project in my region of Pokhara, and by 2011, it had reached 14 regions in Nepal.

WHAT I'M MOST PROUD OF: With this campaign, I managed to mobilize the local population in Nepal to act against global warming. Previous environmental projects had been unsuccessful.

WHAT ROLE DID MY PARENTS PLAY: They helped to plant trees.

WHAT MY FRIENDS THINK: They are impressed!

WHAT I DO NOW: Exhibitions of my paintings are in schools around my city. They encourage children to protect trees and nature.

ANUP RAJ CHALISE

31

BUY REUSABLE CHOPSTICKS TO SAVE THE FORESTS!

QIER QIU, SHANGHAI, CHINA

ACTION: Public awareness and sales of reusable chopsticks.

HOW I'VE CHANGED THE WORLD: An estimated 3,000 people decided to stop using disposable wooden chopsticks.

WHAT I DO NOW: Encourage other young people to join us in our efforts. Or go to other provinces in China to spread the message as widely as possible.

In China, people eat with chopsticks. And millions of people use disposable wooden chopsticks. It may be convenient, but it has an effect on health and the environment.

Disposable chopsticks are made of wood or bamboo. 130 million pairs are manufactured every day. And every day we cut down almost 100 acres of forest—or the equivalent of 55 soccer fields. That's a huge amount of wood that is wasted. In China, deforestation is a serious problem, and the habit of using disposable chopsticks only makes things worse. And on top of that, it's a health hazard. During the process of making the smooth chopsticks, manufacturers use harmful chemicals.

That's what Qier and four of her friends share during their presentations in schools and at other speaking engagements. But just talking about the problem isn't enough.

BACKGROUND
When cutting the trees of the forest, roots that hold soil and allow rain to seep into the ground are destroyed.

People must change their habits. To encourage them to do so, Qier's team offers reusable chopsticks at the end of each of its presentations. Students can buy them and end the habit of using disposable chopsticks. For those who can't afford them, Qier and her friends use a small profit from the sale of the chopsticks to buy chopsticks to give away for free.

QIER QIU

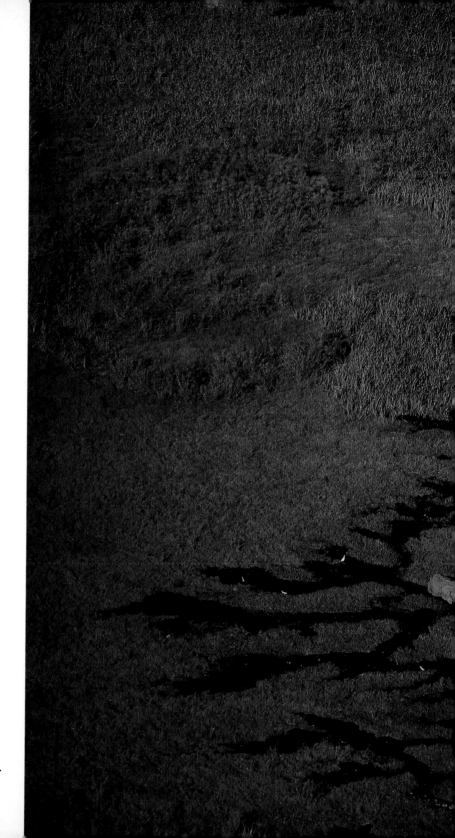

Elephants in Meru
Park, Kenya.

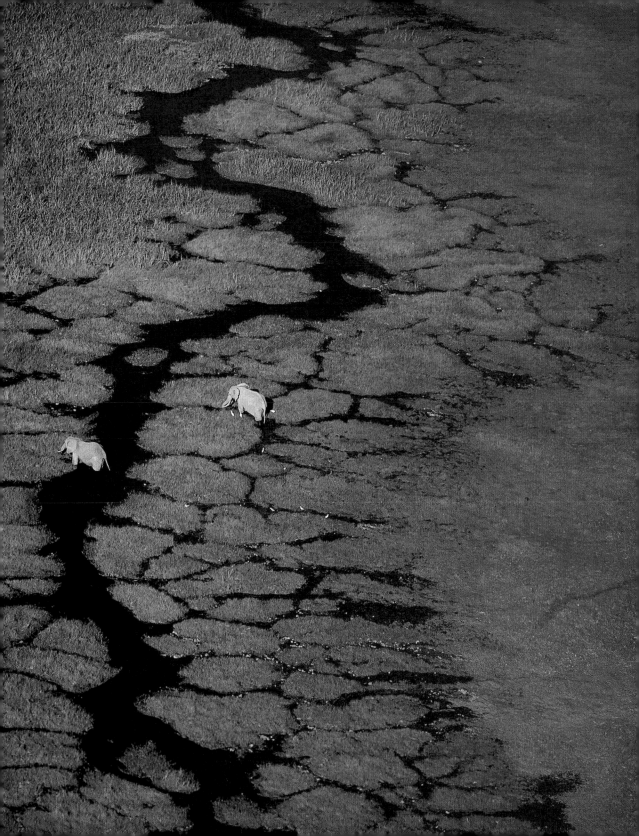

Olivia Bouler

Project Puffin
SEABIRD RESTORATION PROGRAM

I SAVED BIRDS WITH MY PAINTBRUSH.

OLIVIA BOULER, 11 YEARS OLD IN 2010, LIVES IN ISLIP, NEW YORK, UNITED STATES

BACKGROUND

On April 20, 2010, an oil platform exploded in the Gulf of Mexico and caused a gigantic oil spill for the United States and the region.

Imagine your beach vacation, and the waves and rocks and birds. Imagine all that covered with black, sticky oil.

When the disaster happened in the Gulf of Mexico, a black tide of oil covered the beaches of Alabama where Olivia visits her grandparents every year. When she learned what had happened, Olivia became very upset. "I knew it was the breeding season for birds. This was so unfair to them that I started to cry," she said. But soon she decided she couldn't just sit by and do nothing. "I couldn't just watch what was happening without trying to do something about it." So Olivia decided to do what she does best: draw birds! Birds have always fascinated Olivia. "I always wondered how they managed to fly without two engines attached under their wings."

Residue from oil sands in Canada. Oil sands contain oil,
but the process of extracting the oil is highly polluting.

"I KNEW IT WAS THE BREEDING SEASON FOR BIRDS. THIS WAS SO UNFAIR TO THEM."

OLIVIA BOULER

Olivia wrote to the Audubon Society, an organization that works for the protection of nature. Her idea was to sell her watercolor paintings of birds and raise money. She had hoped to raise $500, but had no idea what would happen. Thanks to the media and the Internet, Olivia's project quickly gained attention from people around the United States. Donations began pouring in. Olivia's mother was overwhelmed by the number of e-mails of support sent to her. Olivia continued to paint, and within a year, she had helped raise $200,000 for Gulf recovery efforts.

Some of Olivia's paintings were published in a book she wrote. Proceeds from sales of the book continue to help save the birds.

www.oliviabouler.net

OBJECTIVE: Save the birds.

● ● ● ● ● ● ● ● ● ● ● ● ● ● ● ● ● ● ● ●

ACTION: Fund-raising. People who gave money to the organization to help its efforts received a drawing from Olivia.

HOW I'VE CHANGED THE WORLD: $200,000 was raised to save birds hurt by the oil spill.

WHAT I DO NOW: A traveling exhibition of my paintings tours the country, and some of my paintings are auctioned off to raise funds.

MY MOST HEROIC ACTION: Going to Washington, D.C., and meeting with members of Congress.

MY ADVICE: Everyone can make a difference, even children. If I was able to do something, so can anyone.

WHAT MAKES ME THE HAPPIEST: I love all the messages I get on the Facebook page (Save the Gulf: Olivia's Bird Illustrations). There are over 30,600 fans!

WHAT ROLE DID MY PARENTS PLAY: My mom sent my drawings to the people who donated money. She responded to e-mails and organized interviews.

OLIVIA BOULER

THINK GLOBALLY, EAT LOCALLY!

VICTORIA ROGERS, IRELAND

OBJECTIVE:
Become aware of the benefits of local food production with the slogan, "Think globally," (because transportation of food around the globe contributes to global warming) "eat locally" (because eating locally produced fruits and vegetables is one of the solutions to this problem).

ACTION: Create a vegetable garden at school.

HOW I'VE CHANGED THE WORLD: Our project attracted the attention of other schools after we showed how fun it was to start a garden and reap its benefits.

When we sit down to eat at the table, do we know where our food comes from? Can we say where it was produced? Do we know what fruits and vegetables should normally be in season when we are eating them year-round?

Victoria and her friends wanted to see if they could say "yes" to these questions. To do this, they decided to start a garden at their school. They wanted to experience planting seeds with their own hands, watching the plants grow, harvesting the food, and then preparing and eating a meal.

In addition to their own garden, Victoria's group did other activities to promote local foods. They helped set up another garden at a neighboring kindergarten. They worked with the cooks at their school to use food from the school garden and to indicate that on the daily menu. They organized a "grow the biggest pumpkin" contest at their school. And they invented "bags to plant": homemade bags from recycled materials that included seeds, labels, and instructions to encourage kids to plant vegetables at their homes.

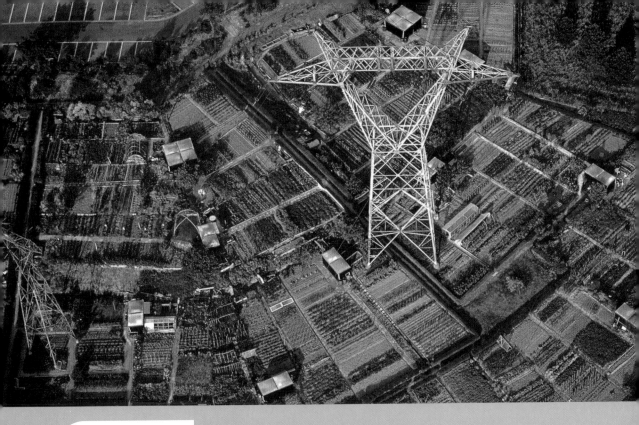

BACKGROUND
Strawberries and green beans grow in summer. When we eat those foods at different times of the year, it's because they have been grown in warm climates in other countries, and then transported to us on airplanes.

With their actions, Victoria and her friends raised awareness of local gardening among students, parents, and government officials. People learned that local food production is good for everyone's health because the food is fresher and richer in vitamins, and good for the planet because less transporting of food reduces pollution. For Victoria and her friends, it's all summed up in one sentence, "Think globally, eat locally."

"PUT YOUR HANDS IN THE EARTH, PLANT SEEDS, WATCH THE PLANTS GROW, HARVEST THE FOOD, AND COOK AND PREPARE A MEAL."

VICTORIA ROGERS

I COLLECTED DATA FOR SCIENCE!

**ANYA SUSLOVA, 13 YEARS OLD IN 2003,
ZHIGANSK, SIBERIA, RUSSIA**

BACKGROUND
The Arctic is a part of the world that warms because of climate change.

In April 2003, an international team of scientists traveled to the Lena River in Siberia. They went to investigate whether climate change was altering the flow of the river and changing the composition of the water. On board the boat that transported them was Anya, the captain's daughter. Although Anya didn't speak English, she was interested in why the scientists had come to her region and what they were planning to do. One part of the project was to take water samples from the river. Anya showed such interest in this process that the scientists gave her twenty bottles at the end of the trip. Because she lived along the river's path, Anya continued collecting water samples. That way data continued to be recorded until the next time the scientists came to visit. With the help of her father, Anya collected samples twice a month and sent the bottles to researchers in the United States. She continued doing this for three years and made a valuable contribution to science.

OBJECTIVE: Contribute to scientific research that will provide a better understanding of the effects of climate change.

ACTION: Collect river water samples for analysis.

HOW I'VE CHANGED THE WORLD: With the data taken from the water samples I collected for three years, the American scientists were able to study the effects of climate change to the Lena River.

Once it was analyzed by scientists, the data from Anya's water samples helped provide important information on how climate change increases or decreases the flow of a river. Scientists decided to extend the scientific study because of their rewarding collaboration with Anya. This became the starting point of the Student Partners Project, a program involving teachers and students in Siberia who help scientists by studying the impact of climate change in the Arctic.

"ANYA'S WORK OVER THREE YEARS HELPED THE SCIENTIFIC COMMUNITY."

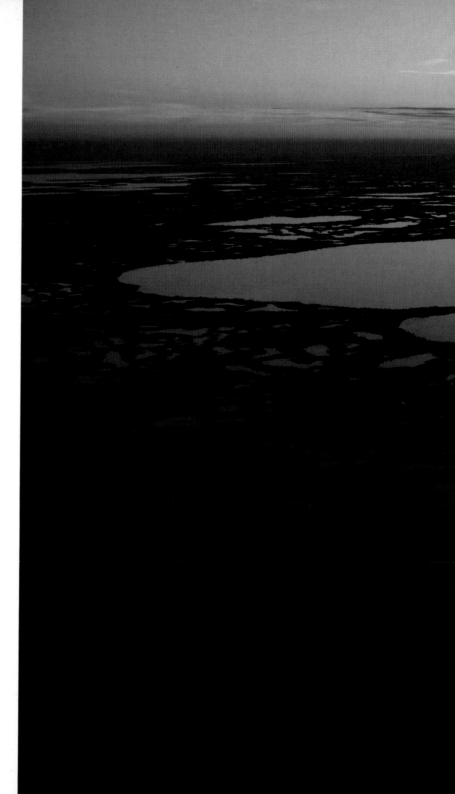

Wetland near Surgut in Siberia, Russia. Permafrost is the top layer of ground that is permanently frozen. It is usually found in northern climates and sometimes in higher altitudes. Its thickness is decreasing quickly because of global warming.

ANYA SUSLOVA

IT'S TIME FOR EVERYONE TO START THINKING ABOUT ECOLOGY.

**JUAN IGNACIO ORDÓÑEZ,
14 YEARS OLD IN 2011, ARGENTINA**

● ● ● ● ● ● ● ● ● ● ● ●

OBJECTIVE: Promote sustainable, green living.

ACTION: Raise awareness.

HOW I'VE CHANGED THE WORLD: Friends and children who live near me have really changed their behavior and now think more about ecology.

WHAT I'M MOST PROUD OF: The positive influence I've had on my friends in my rugby club, the kids at my school, and my family. They've become more environmentally friendly.

WHAT ROLE DID MY PARENTS PLAY: My mother is involved in environmental activities, so she always encouraged me. And my dad thinks what I'm doing is great.

MY ADVICE: The road is long, but you will meet lots of people who are traveling in the same direction and are willing to help you. And when everyone sees the results of their work, they'll be very, very happy!

Where does your desire to act for the environment come from? My mother! She's always had a respect for the environment. At home, we recycle, conserve water, and try to live creating as little waste and litter as possible.

When did you start to become more involved in the environmental movement? In 2008, I participated in a United Nations conference for young people on the environment. Before that, I was already aware of environmental issues, but after the conference I really felt that I could change things.

46

Herd of cattle at a lagoon near Punta Magro, Uruguay.

BACKGROUND
The Rio Summit on the
environment was held
in 1992 . People wanted
to discuss how current
generations could meet
their needs without
limiting the needs of
future generations.

Is there a project that you carried out yourself? In 2011, I proposed an environmental plan for my rugby club. The objective was to adopt green tips to protect the environment, use less energy and water, and reduce waste.

What did you do next? Rio+20 was held in June of 2012. I followed the conference closely because the goal was to present clear and practical ways for people to carry out sustainable development. It's important that young people understand how this works.

JUAN IGNACIO ORDÓÑEZ

WE SAVED THE BOGS.

BERNADETT HEGEDÜS , SCHOOLGIRL,
BUDAPEST, HUNGARY

• •

OBJECTIVE:
Save the last bogs and wild ponds in the Budapest area.

ACTION: Awareness of the issue, using public opinion for support, rehabilitating the natural environment.

HOW I'VE CHANGED THE WORLD: Our initiative helped stop an urbanization project that threatened an area of peatland. And it has made hundreds of people in our area aware of the abundance of nature all around them.

Years ago, the Danube River was surrounded by swamps and bogs (areas of waterlogged grasslands), that were rich in a variety of plant and animal life.

The construction of highways around Budapest destroyed many of the wetlands. To build a mall near Bernadett's school, some ponds were filled in. And then plans were announced to sacrifice a swamp to enlarge the mall's parking lot.

Bernadett and her friends refused to accept this. They created a group, the Green Guards, to create opposition to the plan. The kids didn't have much clout against the powerful adult parking lot planners. But the Green Guards were smart; they spread the message that the bogs and swamps needed to be saved, and they were successful.

Working with a biologist, they now monitor the health of the ponds and measure the mass of sea buckthorn (a typical wetland shrub threatened by invasive plants).

BACKGROUND
Biodiversity loss is when plant or animal species disappear.

The Green Guards participate in lectures about scientific information for the public. They also make presentations in their schools and post information on Internet sites about threatened bogs. Working with the media (newspapers, radio, Internet, television), they are able to communicate to their whole city about any dangers to natural habitats.

The Green Guards also work with students and their parents by replanting cuttings to increase the number of sea buckthorn in the wetlands. Bernadett and her friends have succeeded in stopping the urbanization projects that would have destroyed the remaining peatlands in their area.

BERNADETT HEGEDÜS

Folgefonn Glacier in the highlands of Sørfjorden, Norway. Like most glaciers in the world, Folgefonn's size is diminishing due to global warming.

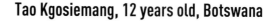

Tao Kgosiemang, 12 years old, Botswana

ACTION: Organize tree plantings with schools and participate in a campaign to eliminate malaria in Africa by distributing mosquito nets. The work is carried out by the Global Youth Alliance Botswana, an association that brings together young people who are motivated to protect the environment.

Kristian Magnus Oien, 12 years old, Norway

ACTION: I recycle used paper at school and at home. I collect litter lying in the schoolyard and in the playground and I throw it in the trash. I like to walk in nature as much as possible to get to know it. I love hiking in the snow and skiing.

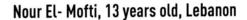

Nour El- Mofti, 13 years old, Lebanon

ACTION: When I was six years old, I was already recycling things and making new projects with them. Today I participate in environmental protection actions like planting trees. I especially work to plant Lebanon cedars because they are the symbol of Lebanon. We've planted about 40,000 trees, but we intend to plant many more.

YOUR VOICE MUST BE HEARD

TA'KAIYA BLANEY, 9 YEARS OLD IN 2010, VANCOUVER, CANADA

● ● ● ● ● ● ● ● ● ● ● ● ● ● ● ● ● ● ●

BACKGROUND
Oil is needed to make gasoline for cars to run on. The oil shipments are transported on boats and through pipelines on land.

When you have a voice you must be heard."

That is Ta'Kaiya's motto, and she isn't afraid to say what she thinks. Or sing what she feels. With the help of her teacher, Ta'Kaiya wrote the song "Shallow Water." The video for the song has been viewed more than 130,000 times, and it has been sung at many music festivals.

But what does Ta'Kaiya say in her song? She speaks of a pipeline that will be built to transport oil across the country. It will run through the land of her Sliammon First Nation ancestors, in the heart of a wild and unspoiled forest. She tells how an oil spill would destroy the shoreline, animals, and the traditions of her people in western Canada, leaving only silence.

"I hope my song will be heard by policymakers in Canada and around the world. My message is to stop the Northern Gateway Pipeline. It crosses over 45 different First Nations territories, putting at risk 45 different cultures and 45 different languages."

Autumn forest in the region of Charlevoix, Quebec, Canada.

"THE PIPELINE AND ITS CONSTRUCTION WILL PROVIDE WORK FOR SOME PEOPLE. BUT IF THERE IS AN ACCIDENT CAUSING AN OIL SPILL, IT WILL LEAVE PEOPLE WITHOUT JOBS AND ALL THE WILDLIFE WILL DIE."

TA'KAIYA BLANEY

In a greater effort to be heard, Ta'Kaiya wrote a letter to all the members of the Parliament of Canada to share her concern. And, with her mother, she went to the offices of Enbridge, the company who wants to build the oil pipeline, to give a letter to the managers. But she was not allowed inside. "I don't know why they are afraid of me. I just wanted them to listen to what I had to say." Maybe it's the truth of what Ta'Kayia sings about that made them afraid?

"I JUST WANTED THEM TO LISTEN TO WHAT I HAD TO SAY."

www.takaiyablaney.com

OBJECTIVE: Prevent the construction of an oil pipeline.

. . . .

ACTION: Educate people in my country and around the world.

HOW I'VE CHANGED THE WORLD: My work contributes to a growing awareness of the problem, and increases the number of people who say "no" to the pipeline.

MY MOST HEROIC ACTION: To go to Enbridge's annual meeting in Calgary, and ask to meet with the CEO Patrick Daniel about why he insists on building the pipeline when so many people are against it.

MY ADVICE: Do everything you can, small things or great things, to save the environment.

WHAT MAKES ME THE HAPPIEST: To know that people have listened to my message, and they are now aware of the problems faced by the environment.

WHAT I AM MOST PROUD OF: When I had the idea of writing the song, I never imagined that one day I would sing at music festivals and even perform at a conference in Indonesia.

WHAT ROLE DID MY PARENTS PLAY: They brought me where I needed to go; they organized my appointments; they helped me prepare my speeches and practice my songs.

I THINK THAT MY FRIENDS: Supported me for the most part. Two good friends feel the same as I do, and they act to protect the environment.

WHAT I DO NOW: Meet and talk to First Nation's children in Canada. I was a delegate at the Earth Summit in Rio de Janeiro in 2012.

TA'KAIYA BLANEY

55

HARMING AN ANIMAL IS NOT THE WAY TO LEARN ABOUT IT!

LAURIE WOLFF, 12 YEARS OLD IN 2001, NEVADA, UNITED STATES

OBJECTIVE:
Defend animals.

ACTION: Petition.

HOW I'VE CHANGED THE WORLD: A new policy at my school allows students to do a virtual dissection of a living creature rather than killing it.

Dissect an animal? Unthinkable for Laurie. Not even a frog. Not even an earthworm. And yet, Laurie found herself with the task of dissecting a worm when she was in the sixth grade. Unwilling to perform the dissection, Laurie asked her teacher to be excused from the exercise. But dissection was mandatory in her biology class. The result was that Laurie, who had excellent grades, received a C. "Cutting an animal in pieces is not the way you learn about it. It's a waste when there are so many other ways to learn about natural sciences without having to kill animals."

Lechwe antelope live in wetland environments.

BACKGROUND
Dissection is used on animals (especially frogs) to learn about anatomy.

Laurie decided to take matters into her own hands. She wrote letters to the principal, the superintendent, and the school board members, spoke with teachers and other students, and led a petition drive. Her hard work paid off two years later, in April of 2002, when the policy of letting students choose whether they wanted to dissect animals or not was implemented.

LAURIE WOLFF

OUR ACTIONS PROTECT THE OCEAN.

MATTHEW SMITH, STUDENT, MADAGASCAR

OBJECTIVE:
Preserve marine biodiversity (the sea and its animals) in Madagascar.

ACTION: Raise public awareness.

HOW I'VE CHANGED THE WORLD:
Our work has helped motivate and educate the Malagasy community, especially young people, about the importance of the environment and the need to protect it.

WHAT I DO NOW: Encourage young people to have a greater respect for the environment.

Imagine a dugong (a large marine mammal) living in a city. And imagine it speaking to a crowd of people. This may sound impossible, but it's not. It is actually one of a number of performance pieces Matthew and his friends have created to explain to the people of Antsiranana, Madagascar, about the threats to the sea and its resources.

Antsiranana Boy Scouts have developed an awareness campaign with the help of C3, an association for the protection of the environment that works directly with the Malagasy people. Using humor, they've written skits and stage plays about the dugong and how it's endangered. Their group performs at public events in the city with the support of the mayor, as well as in schools and colleges. The performances explain to children and young people about the importance of protecting the marine environment.

Whale in the Bay of Samana, Dominican Republic.

BACKGROUND
Dugongs (marine herbivores) are part of the biodiversity in the waters of Madagascar. But their existence is being threatened by human behavior.

To spread the message of their campaign, the scouts offer art workshops, as well as environmental training. They opened an information desk at the University of Antsiranana called the "Resource Center of the Sea" where they welcome young people who wish to learn more about their efforts.

But Matthew and his friends want to do more. To become advocates for marine biodiversity, they would like to create a band of scout "ecoguards." "Ecoguards" are people trained to protect the environment. The scouts would train and teach the guards by using skits and performance pieces.

MATTHEW SMITH

I SPEAK FOR THE WORLD'S KIDS.

YUGRATNA SRIVASTAVA, 13 YEARS OLD, UTTAR PRADESH, INDIA

BACKGROUND
Global warming in India could cause water shortages, famines, and new epidemics.

Yugratna was concerned about the lack of action in addressing the problem of global warming. She had suggestions and recommendations to help the earth's climate. These ideas would lead to a healthier Earth for future generations. But she was frustrated trying to figure out who she should contact with her ideas.

In September of 2009, Yugratna found herself in New York City at the UN Summit on climate change. A hundred heads of state from around the world were there, including the top government leaders from the United States, China, and France. Never before had leaders seen someone so young speak to them from the podium. Yugratna felt it was important for her voice to speak for the three billion children and young people from all over the world.

Since then, Yugratna has delivered speeches to many large gatherings. When she is not in school, she participates in conferences in India and around the world where she talks about climate change and protecting the environment. Yugratna has served as a junior board member for the United Nations TUNZA environment program and vice president of the International Campaign for Plant-for-the-Planet. She believes that we need political action to solve environmental problems.

OBJECTIVE: Promote a lifestyle that respects the environment.

ACTION: Educate the public by speaking at conferences and at schools.

HOW I'VE CHANGED THE WORLD: I started to get involved with environmental projects when I was nine years old and my school joined the Tarumitra organization. It's a student organization that works to promote environmental sensitivity. I believe in motivating young people to help save the environment for future generations.

WHAT I AM MOST PROUD OF: Having world leaders hear the voice of a younger generation.

MY MOST HEROIC ACTION: Speaking to the general assembly of the United Nations in front of 100 heads of state. I was the youngest person to ever do that!

WHAT ROLE DID MY PARENTS PLAY: They have always supported me in everything I've attempted to do.

WHAT MY FRIENDS THINK: They encourage me, and they are happy for me.

MY ADVICE: Be stubborn when you fight for what is right for our future.

WHAT I DO NOW: I dream of planting 200 million trees in India as part of Plant-for-the-Planet. At some time, I'd like to start my own environmental organization.

YUGRATNA SRIVASTAVA

61

A small boat on the Niger River, near Timbuktu. The Niger River flows through nine countries in Africa, and is 2,600 miles long. Nearly 110 million people live along its banks.

THE WHOLE WORLD HAS A RIGHT TO WATER.

RUJUL ZAPARDE, 13 YEARS OLD IN 2007, PLAINSBORO, NEW JERSEY, UNITED STATES

BACKGROUND

Around the world, one in seven people have no access to safe drinking water. Each year 1.4 million children die from diseases brought about by drinking bad water.

How did you get the idea to build a well? In January 2007, I went to visit relatives in Paras, India, which is a rural village. After I arrived, I realized that people didn't have drinking water, and women had to walk several miles twice a day to bring back water. I couldn't believe people had to live like that. Safe drinking water is a right every human being should have. I decided to try and find a way to bring drinking water to villages in India.

How did you make that happen? When I returned from India, I worked on a plan with my friend Kevin. To make our plan a reality, we had to raise $1,000 in order to build a well in the village.

Women at a well near Khudiala, Rajasthan, India.

"WE HAD BAKE SALES AND CAR WASHES, AND AFTER EIGHT MONTHS, WE HAD RAISED THE MONEY. NOW PARAS HAS DRINKING WATER!"

RUJUL ZAPARDE

RUJUL ZAPARDE

What happened after you built the first well? Because we successfully built a well, I was asked if we could build more wells and help other villages. We founded the association Drinking Water for India, and we made presentations at schools in the United States to explain the lack of safe drinking water in India. So far over thirty schools across fourteen states have joined our cause and helped raise money to build new wells.

www.drinkingwaterforindia.org

OBJECTIVE: Bring drinking water to poor villages in India.

ACTION: Raise funds for well construction.

HOW I'VE CHANGED THE WORLD: 47 wells were constructed within four years. That has changed the lives of more than 80,000 villagers.

WHAT ROLE DID MY PARENTS PLAY: At first, my parents were skeptical. They wondered if it would work and whether we could help the situation in a country like India. Now they see what we've accomplished and they support me and my efforts.

WHAT MAKES ME THE HAPPIEST: To see the joy and smiles on the faces of the villagers when clean water starts flowing from a new well.

MY BIGGEST MISTAKE: When I first wanted to motivate students, I contacted school administrators. But they didn't spend much time passing out information, maybe because they didn't want their students distracted by our project. Then we decided to join with environmental clubs that already existed in schools and it worked much better.

MY ADVICE: Even a small action is important. It may not seem like it's having much of an impact, but it's contributing to change.

RUJUL ZAPARDE

67

IN OUR SCHOOL, WE USE WORMS FOR COMPOSTING.

SHALMALI TIWARI, SCHOOLGIRL, INDIA

OBJECTIVE:
Improve waste management.

ACTION: Use vermicomposting in schools.

HOW I'VE CHANGED THE WORLD:
Almost five and a half pounds of compost is harvested daily in our school. In three years, twenty-six schools have joined our vermicomposting campaign. We raised awareness of this through community organizations in our village and made them aware of the benefits of vermicomposting.

More than 122,000 students in 474 schools receive a school lunch every day. In one month, a single school throws away almost 1,000 pounds of lunchtime garbage. Shalmali and her friends knew that the wasted food was polluting the environment. They also learned that a little over four pounds of worms consume more than two pounds of food waste each day. Shalmali realized worms could turn some of this waste into compost, a fertilizer that enriches the soil.

Shalmali and her friends visited the School of Agriculture, where they gave a presentation on vermicomposting. They were asked to see if they could educate villages about the benefits of their work.

Workers in the fields of Jodhpur, India.

BACKGROUND
Organic waste includes fruit and vegetable peels, shells, eggs, etc. Worms can decompose and compost organic waste, which makes a natural fertilizer that feeds plants.

Shalmali and her friends met with village leaders to explain the benefits of vermicomposting and asked for help in getting their message to the people. They also worked with various groups that prepared school meals and told them about the benefits of vermicomposting.

Using the money they made from selling some of the compost, Shalmali's group was able to buy a new gate, fencing, and gardening tools for the school. The rest of the compost was used to feed the trees in the school courtyard.

SHALMALI

MY CITY ENCOURAGES FAIR TRADE.

ANNIE COLLINS, 12 YEARS OLD IN 2008, NAKUSP, BRITISH COLUMBIA, CANADA

• • • • • • • • • • • • • • • • • • • •

BACKGROUND
Fair trade works to support small businesses in poor countries.

What gave you the idea to create an environmental club? When I was in fifth grade, I wanted to do something to help the environment. I was at a conference where I learned about fair trade. So when I started our club, I thought fair trade would be a cause to support. Our first goal was to have Nakusp be known as "Fair Trade Town."

What does that mean? Fair trade cities are committed to helping teach people about fair trade and how important it is for the whole world. To do this, stores need to offer fair trade products and people need to buy them. And everyone—the mayor, government officials, schools, businesses, restaurants, and other associations—should buy fair trade products such as coffee or tea.

What role did your club play? We met with different organizations and presented the benefits of fair trade, encouraged them to participate in the program, and explained how they could do that. We also made presentations to schools to educate students and the entire school community.

And thanks to you, your city was certified as a fair trade town? Yes, thanks to our campaign, Nakusp became the first city certified in British Columbia!

ACTION: Educate businesses, retailers, and city associations.

HOW I'VE CHANGED THE WORLD: In 2009, Nakusp became the first city certified in fair trade in British Columbia.

WHAT ROLE DID MY PARENTS PLAY: They were always there to help me and make my projects possible.

WHAT MY FRIENDS THINK: They are interested in what I do and think it's pretty cool. But because they are so busy, many of them can't get as involved as some of the others.

MY ADVICE: Work to make your dreams happen. Do what interests you and what you really care about. Get advice from people who work in the same field and partner with them to achieve your goals.

WHAT I DO NOW: I started a new project to eliminate disposable plastic bottles at school and encourage students to use reusable metal containers.

ANNIE COLLINS

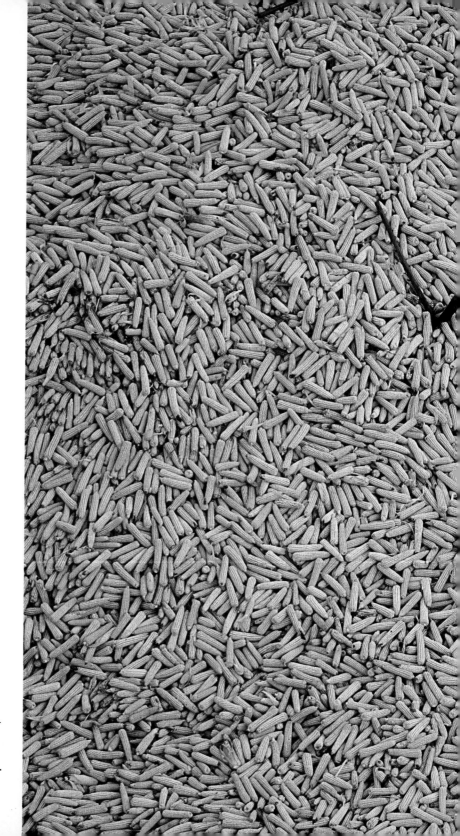

White maize stored for
fair trade usage in Masai
Mara, Kenya.

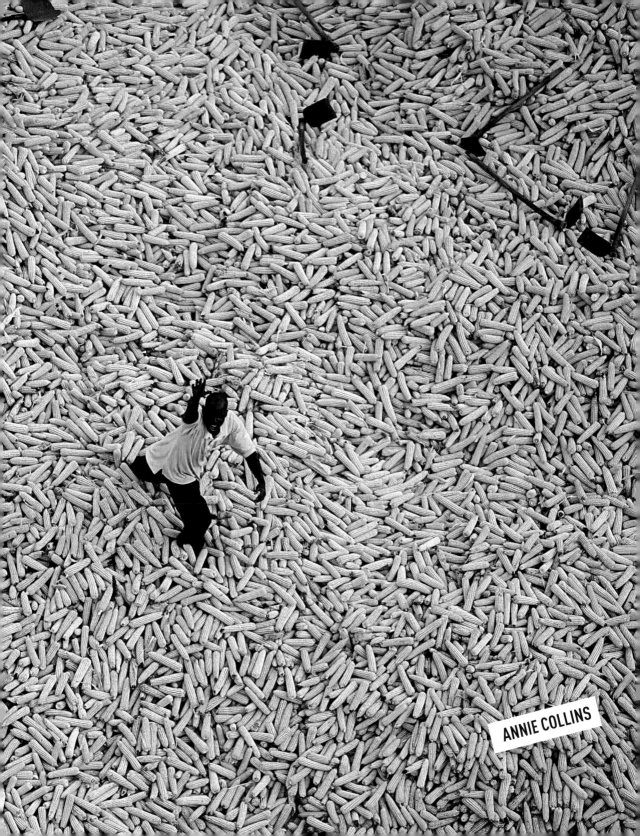

ANNIE COLLINS

ART CAN MAKE PEOPLE STOP AND THINK.

KATHERINE LIU, 12 YEARS OLD, UNITED STATES

• • • • • • • • • • • • • • • • • • • •

OBJECTIVE:
Make the public aware of important environmental problems.

ACTION: Drawing and painting.

They say a beautiful picture is worth a thousand words. For Katherine, it's true.

"Art can get people to think," Katherine says. "But in order for art to communicate a message, it first has to be seen by people."

For several years, Katherine sent her works to an international children's drawing competition organized annually by the United Nations Environment Programme. In 2010, Katherine's piece won second place out of more than 600,000 drawings from hundreds of countries. It showed a train carrying a giraffe, a polar bear, a rhinoceros, and other animals that are endangered. The train arrives at a place where the tracks go in two different directions. In one direction is a safe world using solar- and wind-powered energy. The other direction leads to a sharp cliff. Katherine's drawing suggests people need to think about what will happen to the train and the animals if they choose the wrong track.

74

A wind farm in Middelgrunden, Denmark. Wind turbines now provide almost 20 percent of the country's electricity.

BACKGROUND
The wind and sun provide renewable energy sources.

Katherine works to protect the environment at home and at school. But she wants to do more. Unlike words, a beautiful painting speaks in a language to everyone around the world. Katherine wants her artwork to make people aware of climate change, pollution, and endangered species. At the same time, her drawings also show the positive things people around the world have done for the environment.

KATHERINE LIU

I WANTED TO BE THE YOUNGEST PERSON TO REACH THE NORTH POLE.

PARKER LIAUTAUD, 15 YEARS OLD IN 2010, LONDON, ENGLAND

• •

BACKGROUND
In 2010, 15-year-old Parker attempted to be the youngest person to travel to the North Pole on skis.

What motivated you to try to ski to the North Pole? I created an organization called The Last Degree to inform, inspire, and educate young people about climate change. I thought that being the youngest person to reach the North Pole would make people aware of my organization and its goals.

Why did your first attempt fail? It was unseasonably warm. Open water appeared, and the ice began to drift quickly to the south. Eventually we were evacuated by helicopter. The only positive thing about what happened was that it strengthened our message about the damage caused to the Arctic by global warming. I felt that my mission was really important, so I decided to try again.

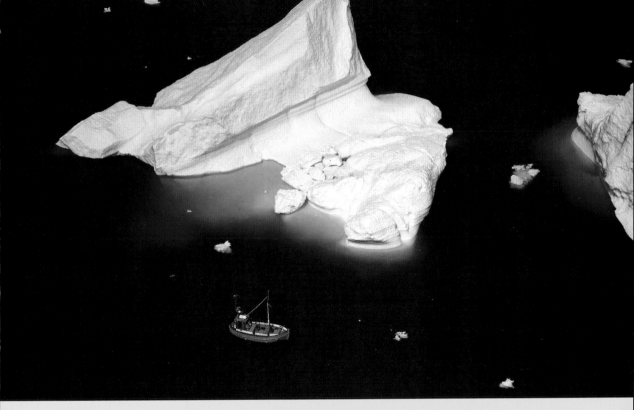

An iceberg floating in Unartoq Fjord, Greenland. Most icebergs that float into Baffin Bay and the Labrador Sea come from the west coast of Greenland. Each year the number of icebergs is estimated to be between 10,000 and 40,000.

"THE ONLY POSITIVE THING ABOUT WHAT HAPPENED WAS THAT IT STRENGTHENED OUR MESSAGE ABOUT THE DAMAGE CAUSED TO THE ARCTIC BY GLOBAL WARMING."

PARKER LIAUTAUD

What happened on your second expedition in April 2011? The temperature was twenty-two degrees below zero, and I was pulling a sled as heavy as me. But my guide Doug Stoup and I were well-trained and highly motivated. It took four days to cover seventy-five miles.

How did you fund your adventure? At first it was very difficult. I had no money, no contacts, no support. I sent about 1,500 letters and e-mails trying to find a sponsor for my project, but everyone turned me down. But I tried again, and the second time it took me four months to raise the funds.

www.parkerliautaud.com

OBJECTIVE:

Encourage young people to find ways to reduce greenhouse gas emissions.

• •

HOW I'VE CHANGED THE WORLD: Tens of thousands of young people followed my expedition and learned about climate change through my website The Last Degree.

WHAT MAKES YOU HAPPIEST: The success of my second attempt showed people that I could achieve my goals.

WHAT I'M MOST PROUD OF: Having managed to find the financing for the first and second expeditions because it was kind of a "mission impossible."

WHAT ROLE DID YOUR PARENTS PLAY: They supported me when I had challenges. But I managed to arrange all the financing on my own and without their help. I wanted to be independent, and I think that was a good choice because it showed people I was entirely responsible for my project.

MY ADVICE: Do a good job of presenting your project and read what people are saying about it. People will see you care and that you want to accomplish something.

WHAT I DO NOW: I've made two more treks to the North Pole. I'm also an ambassador for One Young World, an organization that gathers together young people from around the world, helping them make lasting connections to create positive change.

PARKER LIAUTAUD

WE ARE ALL FRIENDS OF NATURE.

ADELINE SUWANA,
12 YEARS OLD IN 2008, INDONESIA

• • • • • • • • • • • • • • •

BACKGROUND
Global warming will affect the climate of the Earth. For example, there will be more floods and droughts.

OBJECTIVE:
Slow down the deterioration of the environment and inspire children to preserve nature.

ACTION: Plant trees, help the ocean's coral reefs, speak at conferences, and give tours of national parks.

HOW I'VE CHANGED THE WORLD:
Through my work, thousands of children have been encouraged to love nature and to act to protect it.

In 2007, Adeline's village was devastated by a flooded river. Adeline's family had to be evacuated. Adeline wondered what could cause such a serious flood. In her research, she learned that the earth's climate was changing, and plants and animal species were disappearing. She decided to act with other children to protect the environment. On her next summer vacation, she banded together with friends to replant a mangrove forest that protected the coastline and offered protection for fish. It was the starting point for a movement that would become more and more important. Adeline founded Sahabat Alam, a nonprofit organization that aims to nurture young people's love and awareness of the environment, and to encourage them at an early age to become involved with environmental actions. Sahabat Alam has more than 1,700 members throughout Indonesia. Their diverse activities include revitalizing coral reefs, monitoring turtle and marine life, and picking up litter on beaches.

Floods in November of 2011 stranded vehicles on a highway near Khu Bang Luang, Thailand. The floods lasted for long periods of time and were responsible for more than five hundred deaths. The floods were especially bad for the twelve million residents in the capital of Bangkok and its surrounding area.

For Adeline, the most important thing to do is pass on the message of "Save the Planet." She does this by educating children, taking tours through national parks, and visiting schools. She speaks to students about the importance of protecting nature and sharing ideas that will help them meet that goal.

http://sahabat-alam.com/en/

ADELINE SUWANA

THE INTERNET CAN HELP THE WHOLE WORLD.

DYLAN MAHALINGAM, 9 YEARS OLD IN 2004, DERRY, NEW HAMPSHIRE, UNITED STATES

● ● ● ● ● ● ● ● ● ● ● ● ● ● ●

OBJECTIVE:
Contribute to reducing poverty.

ACTION: Create a website to inform people about worldwide poverty and fund-raise for the cause.

HOW I'VE CHANGED THE WORLD:
We raised $780,000 to help tsunami victims in Asia in 2004. We collected $10 million in 2005 for people after Hurricane Katrina hit the United States. Since then more than $70,000 in donations have been raised for different projects that have improved the lives of one million children around the world.

One day, Dylan's parents told him that the uneaten food on his plate could feed a family for a week in a poor country. "I wondered how I could carry my plate of food to another child somewhere else in the world," Dylan remembers. Dylan felt he should do something for children living in poverty. He learned about the Millennium Development Goals (MDGs) organized by the United Nations Development Programme. Dylan decided to take action and founded Lil'MDGs. Lil'MDGs goal is to inform, inspire, engage, and empower the world's children to help solve serious local and global issues.

A flooded house south of Dhaka, Bangladesh.

BACKGROUND

In 2000, the United Nations listed eight objectives called the Millennium Development Goals to reach by 2015. The first is to reduce poverty and hunger around the world.

For each of the eight MDGs, the Lil'MDGs website explains how to contribute by donating money or sending books and school supplies. "Children want to help the poor, but they don't know how. It's more fun and less intimidating for them to donate money with technology, like the Internet. More than 3 million children across 41 countries have already contributed to Lil'MDGs projects. The organization works with the Jayme's Fund foundation, which manages the money that is collected. The donations raised by Lil'MDGs have helped build many things, including a dormitory at a school in Tibet, a library and a mobile hospital in India, and a recreation center in Uganda.

DYLAN MAHALINGAM

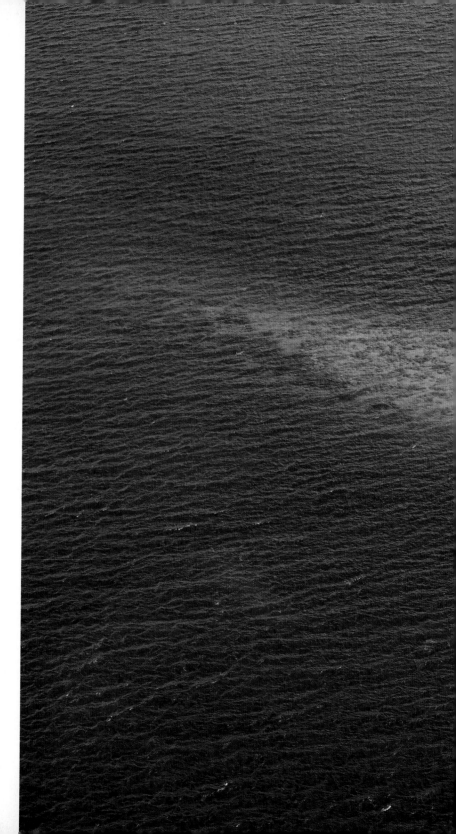

The homes of the Kuna people in the Robeson Islands, San Blas archipelago, Panama. The 400,000 people living on a series of small islands are threatened by rising sea levels.

Rhiannon Tomtishen and Madison Vorva, 16 years old, United States

Our action for the planet: Make people aware of the damage done by palm oil plantations.

Our work started after we made two discoveries. The first was that orangutans were disappearing in southeast Asia, particularly because their forests were being destroyed and replaced by palm oil plantations. And the second was that the cookies that members of the Girl Scouts USA sell every year contain palm oil. Because we are Girl Scouts, we wanted to launch a campaign to raise public awareness of the problem. Working with the Rainforest Action Network and the Union of Concerned Scientists, we organized a petition for people to sign to send to the leaders of the Girl Scouts. The result was that over 70,000 e-mails were sent, and we were able to meet with the leaders of the Girl Scouts. They've said they are committed to working with palm oil plantations that do not destroy rain forests, and they will explore replacing palm oil with other edible oils.

Sebastian Jaime and Rivero Davila, 12 years old, Bolivia

Action: Have the students in my school participate in global environmental efforts.

Working with Plant-for-the-Planet, I encouraged children living on the Andean Plateau to plant trees. I also helped organize a march to make young people aware of environmental problems such as air pollution.

Amala Desarathi, 15 years old, Bangalore, India

Action: Set up a sorting and recycling site in my city of Bangalore.

When an organization began to educate people in my neighborhood about recycling, I immediately wanted to help out. When I joined the group, I was the youngest member. I focused on talking with young people about the importance of sorting trash and seeing what can be recycled. The first recycling center was set up in an area where 250 people live. I hope that by working with other kids, we can have centers throughout our city.

TREES ARE LIFE.

**MAIKEN HAMALUBA,
11 YEARS OLD IN 2008, BOTSWANA**

OBJECTIVE:
Fight against desertification in Africa. Desertification is when a dry land region becomes even dryer when it loses what little water areas it has.

ACTION: Reach out to schools and plant trees.

HOW I'VE CHANGED THE WORLD: I've shown young people what they can do despite their age. Most people think that because we're young, we can't change the world. I proved them wrong!

WHAT MAKES ME THE HAPPIEST: Knowing that the results of the work I've done will live on in the future and improve people's lives.

HOW ARE YOUR PARENTS INVOLVED? My father manages the finances.

WHAT DO YOUR FRIENDS THINK? They are always happy to help me when I need it. They believe, as I do, that to preserve our land we must all work together.

MY ADVICE: You're never too young to change the world!

Why did you decide to plant trees? Because trees are life. We know they create the air we breathe. But they are also essential for daily life: they provide wood for cooking, heating, building homes, and making paper. And trees provide shade for everyone!

How did you let people know about your tree planting campaign? My father and I prepared and distributed fliers to make people aware of the problem of desertification and to promote our project. It was featured on a radio program. And I worked with ENO (Environment Online), an environmental education association which works with schools in more than 100 countries around the world. I used their newsletter to write about the importance of reforestation in Botswana. More than 100 ENO schools in Africa received the newsletter.

An area of deforestation in Maroantsetra Toamasina, Madagascar.

BACKGROUND
In Africa, wood is often the only energy source available for cooking and heating water. In semi-desert countries with little water, vegetation struggles to grow and stay alive.

How did you find the money to buy plants and planting tools? I received financial aid from the We Are Family Foundation in the United States to support and encourage our actions.

What results have you achieved? Our campaign has helped plant more than 2,500 trees in Botswana. I also visit schools to tell students about why we must preserve trees for our future, and to encourage them to plant trees themselves. I've made almost 150 presentations to over 10,000 students.

MAIKEN HAMALUBA

STOP TALKING. START PLANTING!

FELIX FINKBEINER,
9 YEARS OLD IN 2007, GERMANY

• • • • • • • • • • • • • • • • • • •

BACKGROUND

Carbon dioxide is a gas that disrupts the planet's atmosphere. Green plants consume carbon dioxide as they grow and release oxygen.

In preparing a report on climate change using the CM1 computer program for atmospheric research, Felix learned that trees reduce global warming. An idea occurred to him: what if the children of the world acted as a global family and planted trees? At the end of the class presentation of his report, Felix asked a question of his fellow students: "What if we could get people to plant one million trees in every country in the world?"

Felix knew if his plan was to succeed, he would have to motivate other children. Two months later, the first tree was planted at his school. Aided by his school's support, he launched a website that included a counter that recorded the number of trees being planted.

Storm over the Amazon rain forest near Téfé, Brazil.
Covering 2,100,000 square miles, the Amazon is the
largest rain forest in the world.

"I HAD THE IDEA THAT CHILDREN COULD PLANT TREES. THE CHILDREN OF THE WORLD COULD ACT TOGETHER LIKE A BIG GLOBAL FAMILY!"

FELIX FINKBEINER

FELIX FINKBEINER

In 2009, Felix attended a conference and taught a class entitled, "Plant-for-the-Planet." Participating schools sent students between the ages of ten and twelve. During a day of information and training, the children learned about the art of planting trees. They were also taught how to give public presentations that would encourage other children to support their project. "This way, our movement will be unstoppable as it continues to grow," said Felix. Since then, over 140 student presentations have been held in twenty countries involving more than 12,000 kids.

The project has become such a success that only three years after Felix's first presentation, four million new trees had been planted around the world, including one million in Germany.

Today, Plant-for-the-Planet has become an internationally recognized foundation with the slogan "Stop talking. Start planting."

"FOUR MILLION NEW TREES ARE GROWING AROUND THE WORLD."

www.plant-for-the-planet.org

OBJECTIVE: Limiting global climate change.

• •

ACTION: Planting trees.

HOW I'VE CHANGED THE WORLD:
Since I started my project, four million trees have been planted in more than 100 countries throughout the world by more than 100,000 children.

WHAT MAKES ME THE HAPPIEST:
Having succeeded in motivating thousands of children to plant trees.

WHAT I 'M MOST PROUD OF: I got to meet Wangari Maathai of Kenya, who started a campaign in 2006 that planted 12.5 billion trees worldwide. She inspired me a lot. Upon her death in September 2011, the United Nations asked the children of Plant-for-the-Planet to continue her work and plant trees around the world. It's a big responsibility that the adults have given us.

MY ADVICE: We, the children, can be found everywhere around the world. If we all act together, we can really change things. A mosquito can't do anything to a rhinoceros, but a thousand mosquitoes can force a rhino to change direction.

WHAT I DO NOW: Governments around the world refuse to work together to act against climate change. This is terrible. So we will create the first global political party, which will exist in every country of the world and will act together to create change.

FELIX FINKBEINER

93

The Banc d'Arguin National Park, in Gironde, France. It is a winter nesting area for many species of migratory birds, including a colony of 4,000 pairs of terns. This colony is one of the three largest in Europe.

Helga Anfinsen, 12 years old, Norway

MY ACTION FOR THE PLANET: I attend a school that participates in positive environmental activities. At school, trash and garbage are recycled. Our school also helped rehabilitate a river and a swamp, which allowed salamanders and insects to repopulate the area.

I am a member of the Norwegian Hiking Association, the largest association in the country that participates in outdoor activities while respecting nature.

Jin Ho Huh, 13 years old, South Korea

Action: Make your own reusable bags out of recycled materials. That way, we use fewer disposable bags and it encourages recycling.

Eleanor Sutcliffe, 11 years old, Wales, United Kingdom

Action: My project is SOS: Save Our Seas. Our goal is to clean up the ocean beaches in a particular region. A group of people meet weekly and pick up trash washed up on shore. Everything that is collected is noted and recorded. Then the information is sent to the Marine Conservation Society, an association for the protection of the marine environment, to provide facts for their environment database.

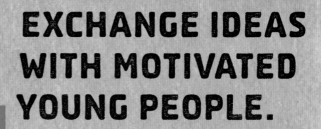

EXCHANGE IDEAS WITH MOTIVATED YOUNG PEOPLE.

JAHMALI BRIDGEWATER,
10 YEARS OLD IN 2008, BERMUDA

OBJECTIVE:
Encourage young people to change their daily behavior so they have a positive impact on the environment.

ACTION: Start an environmental awareness club at my school.

HOW I'VE CHANGED THE WORLD: More people are aware of the simple things they can do to protect the environment.

WHAT MAKES ME THE HAPPIEST: I started the Green Kids Club at my school. When I graduated to a new school, I thought that might be the end of the club. But there are a bunch of kids who keep the club running. It gives me hope.

MY ADVICE: Try to participate in nature activities.

When he was younger, Jahmali's family had no television. So Jahmali spent hours outdoors exploring nature. With guidebooks in hand, he discovered the flora and fauna of Bermuda. At school, he founded The Green Kids Club, a nature club made up of other kids who were interested in the environment. The club organized a field trip for students to visit a recycling center, and it conducted a study to determine whether their school was environmentally friendly. Because of his efforts, Jahmali was selected to represent his school at a conference on children and the environment, organized by the National Zoo and Aquarium of Bermuda in 2008. The event included a writing contest to select two winners to go to Norway to attend the Annual UN Youth meeting on the environment. One of the winners was Jahmali! Upon his return from Norway, Jahmali wrote a report about what he had learned at the conference. The Bermuda environment minister was so impressed that he met with Jahmali and provided assistance for Jahmali to attend the 2009 meeting in South Korea. And the following year, Jahmali again attended the conference, this time in Japan.

Great Blue Hole, Lighthouse Reef Atoll, Belize.

BACKGROUND
Each year the UN Environment Programme organizes a conference for the young people of the world.

These gatherings bring together young people, like Jahmali, who are concerned about the future of the planet. At the conferences, people share ideas and stories from around the world.

Inspired by these events, and eager to share his experiences with the children of Bermuda, Jahmali wrote *Growing Green**, a book in which he gives tips for living with less impact on the environment. Some of these tips include limiting energy use, reducing the amount of waste you create, replacing lightbulbs with low energy bulbs, planting trees, and other ideas.

JAHMALI BRIDGEWATER

* *Growing Green (My Environmental Journey)*, Jahmali Bridgewater, Xlibris, 2010.

IF I DON'T TAKE A STAND TO SAVE THE GORILLAS, WHO WILL?

JAMES BROOKS, 9 YEARS OLD IN 2005, LONDON, CANADA

• •

BACKGROUND

In Africa and Asia, apes, our closest cousins, are disappearing because they are being killed by poachers for their meat. In addition, the tropical forests where they live are being cut down and destroyed.

What inspired you to take action to save the great monkeys? I've always loved chimpanzees, bonobos, gorillas, and orangutans. There are so many ways in which they are like humans. But their homes and habitats are being threatened. In twenty years, some of them will disappear if nothing is done.

What information is available on your website www. apeaware.org? ApeAware provides information on all kinds of apes and lets people know how and why they are threatened. I designed the site for both children and adults.

You also support the Canadian Ape Alliance, an association for the protection of great apes? Yes, this organization has projects located in places like the Democratic Republic of Congo. Their efforts there are to help protect the gorillas of Kahuzi–Biega by supporting park rangers in their fight against poachers. They also work to improve the living conditions of the guards' families.

Palm oil plantation in Borneo, Indonesia. Harvesting palm oil is the main cause of deforestation in Indonesia. This oil is used in many food products.

"I WANTED MY ACTIONS TO LEAD TO A REAL IMPROVEMENT IN THE LIVES OF THE PEOPLE AND GORILLAS IN THE CONGO."

JAMES BROOKS

Our efforts require funding for the Canadian Ape Alliance. One of the projects, Eggs for Kids, is partially funded by the program 1,000 Classrooms. Each of the classrooms donates three dollars to Eggs for Kids. With the money, we set up a poultry farm for mothers in the Congo. The farms supply nutritious eggs for their children, and it teaches the women how to run a small business. In addition, the students in 1,000 Classrooms are made aware of the problems for apes in Africa.

www.apeaware.org

www.1000classrooms.org

OBJECTIVE: Save the great apes.

ACTION: Create awareness and start fund-raising.

HOW I'VE CHANGED THE WORLD: $6,200 was collected and 25,000 eggs were purchased. The initial objective was $3,000, and it was reached in one year!

WHAT MAKES ME THE HAPPIEST: To see that there are a lot of children ready to help. It made me happy to see them care about the disappearance of the apes.

WHAT I 'M MOST PROUD OF: I wanted my actions to lead to a real improvement in the lives of the people and gorillas in the Congo.

MY MOST HEROIC ACTION: The number of conferences I attended. In the beginning, I had difficulties pronouncing some words and it made me nervous to speak in public. But I told myself, "If I don't take a stand to save the gorillas, who will?"

WHO HELPED YOU: Many friends helped me and made small donations even when they weren't as involved as I was in the organization.

MY ADVICE: Find people who have the same concerns as you do, and work with them. In my case, two associations (Canadian Ape Alliance and Bonobo Conservation Initiative) have given me help and inspiration.

WHAT I DO NOW: My current project is an Action Reforestation in the Democratic Republic of the Congo, to develop the Kokolopori Forest where bonobos live.

JAMES BROOKS

101

Ipanema Beach, Rio de Janeiro, Brazil. About 14 billion pounds of garbage is thrown into the ocean each year by human beings.

IT'S TIME TO SAVE EARTH.

**HANAN HASSAN AND JULIA LIN,
10 YEARS OLD IN 2011, SYDNEY, AUSTRALIA**

OBJECTIVE:
Reduce our impact on the planet by changing our behavior.

ACTION: Start a club to get students to think about the effect they have on our planet. Encourage them to make positive changes at school as well as at home.

WHAT MAKES US HAPPY: It was cool to win the Earth Hour's 2011 Young Panda Award, which is awarded annually for kid's positive environmental activities!

WHAT WE DO NOW: We installed solar panels and a rainwater tank on the roof of our school.

Imagine a green school where students save energy, recycle, and use the sun to provide electricity. Hanan and Julia have done more than imagine doing this; they've acted on it. With some friends and the help of their science teacher, they founded a club in 2009 called EnviroKids. Their goal was to invite students and teachers to try an ecologically friendly life style. The way to do this was through weekly meetings to discuss environmental issues and to plan what actions needed to be taken.

To reduce waste, the club placed containers for the class to deposit sheets of paper used on one side, and other containers for paper recycling. On Friday they had a "zero waste" lunch where students were encouraged to avoid using any disposable packaging or containers. There was also a day dedicated to tree planting in which the whole school participated. A gardening club was created to cultivate the school garden and install a site to turn waste into green compost.

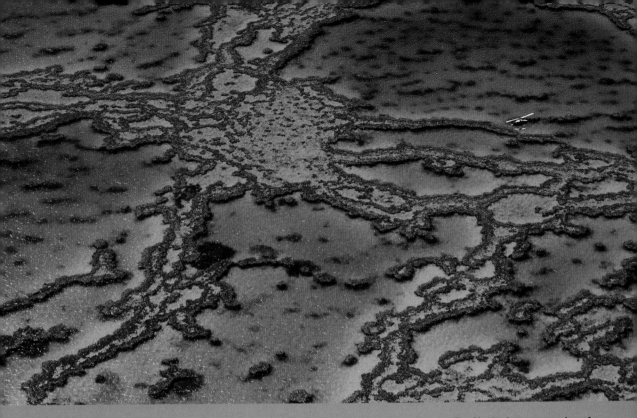

The Great Barrier Reef, Australia. About 135,000 square miles, the Great Barrier Reef is the largest coral reef system in the world. It is home to 400 species of coral, 1,500 species of fish, and 4,000 species of mollusks.

BACKGROUND
Earth Hour was an event that first took place in Sydney Australia, in 2007. 2.2 million people turned off nonessential lights for one hour to raise awareness about climate change.

In March 2011, Hanan and Julia wanted to do more for the Earth Hour campaign than just turn off lights for an hour. Inspired by EnviroKids, their whole school spent one week turning off lights, computers, fans, and air conditioners that weren't needed. And on the last day, two hours of class were held outdoors.

Hanan and Julia were honored for their environmental work with Earth Hour's Young Panda Award, which recognizes young people who are doing outstanding work to fight against global warming.

HANAN HASSAN AND JULIA LIN

WHEN I THINK OF THE ARCTIC, I THINK AS AN INUIT.

AINHOA HARDY, 14 YEARS OLD IN 2008, GREENWICH, CONNECTICUT, UNITED STATES

• • • • • • • • • • • • • • • • • • • •

BACKGROUND
The Pax Arctica Initiative (Peace in the Arctic) promotes awareness of environmental threats to the Arctic.

What was your role in the children's trip to the Arctic? Nine of us between the ages of nine and seventeen from Europe, the United States, and Africa made the journey. We went to see the changes happening to the Arctic because of global warming, and then report back on what we discovered. We surveyed, took photographs, and measured glaciers.

What effect did this visit to the Arctic have on you? Most people think that the Arctic is a completely frozen region. I discovered that it's a very diverse place, with an abundance of wildlife and plant life. When I think of the Arctic now, I think of the Inuit people who live there and who shared their culture with us. Global warming touches these people who need ice and animals in order to have homes and food.

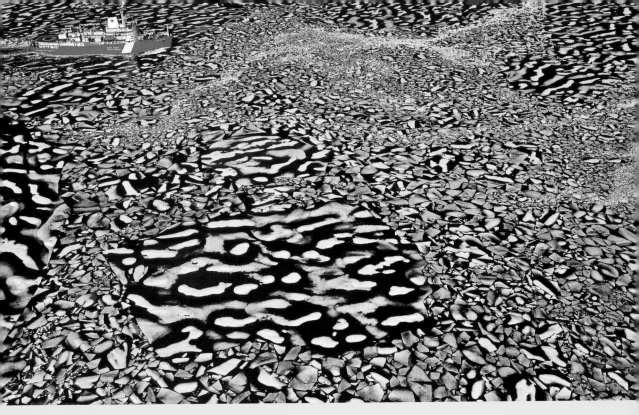

An icebreaker boat in Resolute Bay, Canada. The Arctic region is rapidly warming. At the current rate, the ice could disappear by 2050.

"THIS WASN'T A NEWSPAPER ARTICLE OR A TELEVISION PROGRAM. THESE WERE REAL PEOPLE WHOSE LIVES WERE BEING THREATENED BECAUSE OF GLOBAL WARMING."

AINHOA HARDY

How did you serve as Arctic Ambassador after your return?
I organized presentations at my school, and I showed photos
and videos to my friends. I was interviewed for newspapers
and magazines to talk about the Arctic expedition. A book
was published to publicize our adventure: *Arctic Transitions*
by Luc Hardy.

Was this your first expedition? No, when I was 12, I
climbed Mount Kilimanjaro in Africa with my father. It was
a big physical and mental challenge, but there was a terrific
reward in the end. I was able to raise $10,000 in donations
for the Save Darfur organization to help the Darfur region
in the Sudan War.

OBJECTIVE: Make the public aware of the changes that threaten the Arctic.

. . . .

ACTION: Join the Arctic expedition with eight other young people.

HOW I'VE CHANGED THE WORLD: I gave speeches and presentations at my school to 300 students, from sixth-graders up to seniors. I think I helped them become aware of the reality of global warming because here was someone standing in front of them who had seen the changes that were taking place. It wasn't the same as if they just read an article in the newspaper or saw a program on the television.

WHAT ROLE DID MY PARENTS PLAY: My father was one of the organizers of the trip. He gave me the chance to participate in an amazing adventure, and I am grateful for that.

WHAT I AM MOST PROUD OF: Our group was able to report back about the effects of global warming on the Ward Hunt ice shelf, the largest floating platform of ice in the Arctic.

I THINK THAT MY FRIENDS: would like to join me on my expeditions!

MY ADVICE: Don't wait for someone else to act first. We must learn what we can do now for the environment. When there are government elections, we should ask adults to vote for candidates who are supporting efforts to preserve the environment.

AINHOA HARDY

WHEN I'M FIGHTING FOR SHARKS, I'M FIGHTING FOR ALL OF US.

ONDINE ELIOT, 12 YEARS OLD IN 2008, LIVES IN NEUVILLE-SUR-AUNEUIL, OISE, FRANCE

● ● ● ● ● ● ● ● ● ● ● ● ● ● ● ● ● ● ● ●

BACKGROUND

An estimated 73 million sharks are killed each year. Several species are at risk of disappearing.

What are you doing to protect nature? Ever since I can remember, I've loved animals. One day, I was reading a magazine, and I saw horrible pictures of massacred sharks. They showed sharks being caught and then thrown back alive into the ocean after their fins had been cut off to make shark fin soup, a popular dish in Asia. I didn't think people could kill animals with such cruelty. So I decided to start a blog to let people know.

How did your parents react? At first, I didn't say anything. When they discovered my blog, they were very surprised. Then my father helped me to take my message further by creating a display about sharks with nine panels of pictures and information. I traveled around France and did thirty presentations. The first time was in 2009 at a diving school. I contacted the director of the school to see if I could present there and she immediately said yes.

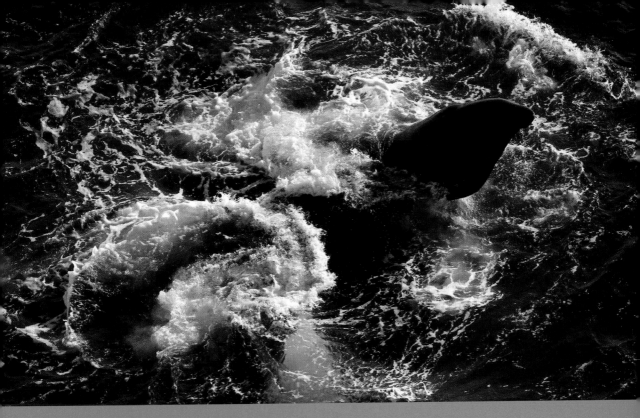

Whale off the coast of Table Mountain National Park in
South Africa.

"WE KILL 73 MILLION SHARKS
EACH YEAR. SOME OF THE
SPECIES WILL SOON DISAPPEAR."

ONDINE ELIOT

How do you raise travel money so you can give your presentations? I met a group of women who have a clothing brand for divers. I told them about my efforts, and they offered to sell a line of T-shirts to support me. I made a drawing: a silhouette of a shark. For each T-shirt that's sold, I get paid $6.50. So far I've raised $1,300, which funded a weeklong event at my school in support of sharks.

Is it difficult to ask for support for an animal that has a scary reputation? At first it was difficult to find the right language to talk about sharks. But after three years, I've become really comfortable speaking about them. And when I fight for sharks, I'm fighting for all species.

"I'M FIGHTING FOR ALL SPECIES."

http://passiondesrequins.skyrock.com/

OBJECTIVE: Save the sharks.

• • • • • • • • • • • • • • • • • • •

ACTION: Inform and raise awareness.

HOW I'VE CHANGED THE WORLD: Through my display, "It Sucks for Sharks," thousands of people have learned that sharks are important for the balance of nature in oceans, but they are threatened.

WHAT I DO NOW: I continue to speak to children in schools in France.

WHAT I AM MOST PROUD OF: Having presented "It Sucks for Sharks" to the kids at my school, and getting such a positive reaction from everyone.

MY ADVICE: It's not enough to have an idea. If you really believe in something, and act on it, you can go far.

WHAT MAKES ME THE HAPPIEST: When I'm giving speeches to strangers and they come up afterward to thank me for my determination to do something for sharks.

WHAT MY FRIENDS THINK: They encourage me and tell me they would never be able to do what I do. But I tell them they can. Three of my friends now join me for school visits.

NO SKIING ON SACRED MOUNTAINS.

ALBERTA NELLS, 16 YEARS OLD IN 2006, FLAGSTAFF, ARIZONA, NATION OF THE NAVAJO, UNITED STATES

OBJECTIVE:
Prevent the expansion of the Arizona Snowbowl ski resort, as well as the use of treated wastewater in making artificial snow.

ACTION: Organized marches and peaceful protests and demonstrations with young people.

WHAT MAKES ME THE HAPPIEST: At first I found it really difficult to speak in public. But as I built up my confidence, I began to speak from the heart, and speaking became as natural to me as breathing. What's funny is that people would come up and say, "Thank you! Thank you for what you said!" But what I was thinking was, "Oh boy, what did I say?" Because when I'm speaking from the heart, I don't always remember what I said.

MY ADVICE: Never give up. Even when you're tired or stressed, keep fighting. Because after a while you'll make people aware of new ideas and you'll start to see the results of your efforts.

When Alberta looks at the San Francisco Peaks that lie north of Flagstaff, Arizona, she sees her grandmother.

In the Indian culture, the San Francisco Peaks are sacred, and for Alberta, they are like a member of her family. For the owners of the nearby ski resort though, the mountains are something to be developed further. At the end of 2002, the owners planned to enlarge the ski area by destroying the neighboring forest. They also planned to make artificial snow from treated wastewater from the city of Flagstaff's Wastewater Treatment Plant. For Alberta and thirteen other Native American Nations for whom the mountains are sacred, the project would spoil their sanctuary. Despite protests, the Forest Service approved the ski resort's plans in 2005.

Immediately, a battle ensued in court between the opponents of the project and the Forest Service. Alberta decided to lead Youth of the Peaks, a group created to the alert the region's young people about the effort to save the mountains.

Monument Valley Park in the United States. The Navajo Nation population is 300,000, including 174,000 people who live on the reserve. Like the other 563 tribes recognized by the federal government of the United States, the Navajo have their own government.

BACKGROUND
Snow is made from sewage treated at a waste management center.

They organized peaceful protest marches on foot and on horseback. Alberta spoke in public to explain to young people that harming the San Francisco Peaks would be a loss to their culture. To make people connect even more with the mountains, Youth of the Peaks provided information about the traditions of the Native Nations people.

The lawsuit lasted several years, until the Supreme Court ruled in favor of the Forest Service in 2009. Protests to the expansion of the ski resort continue to this day.

ALBERTA NELLS

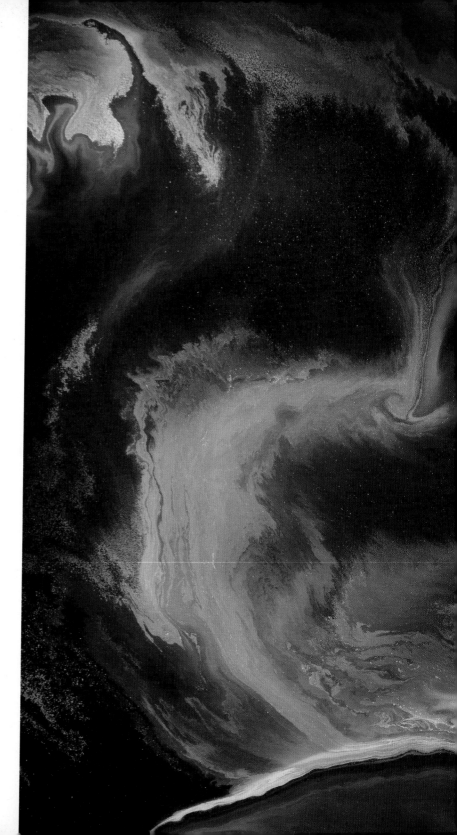

Flamingos flying above crystal formations in Lake Magadi in Kenya.

116

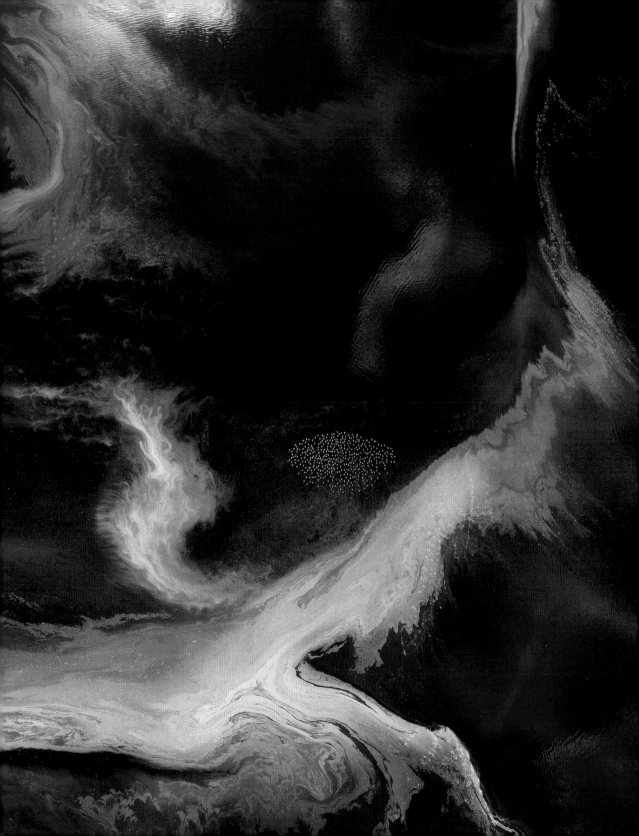

ON STAGE, IT TAKES FIFTEEN MINUTES TO SHARE MY MESSAGE.

**JES ISMAEL IZAIDIN, 15 YEARS OLD IN 2012,
KUALA LUMPUR, MALAYSIA**

- -

OBJECTIVE:
Prevent the disappearance of the Asian tigers.

ACTION: Through a dance, educate the public about the dangers facing Asian tigers.

What was your journey that led you to dancing on stage costumed as a tiger in a piece called "The Phantom Tiger"? I've been interested in the environment since I was seven years old, and art has always fascinated me. I was part of the theater club at my elementary school. Every year, we performed a new piece about an endangered animal. We were trying to raise awareness and money for a good cause.

How was the Tree Theatre Group founded? My father realized that children loved acting and dancing in the animal awareness pieces. In 2006, he created the Tree Theatre Group. TTG raises awareness of environmental issues through theater and dance. What we do is more effective than a two-hour performance. Our piece runs fifteen minutes. That way we are able to directly connect with the audience to convey our message.

http://treetg.com/aboutus.html

Workers in the fields north of Phuket, Thailand.

BACKGROUND
In Asia, tigers are disappearing. Deforestation and illegally cutting down trees is destroying the fields where the tigers live.

What is the message of "The Phantom Tiger"? It is a dance piece that explains the dramatic situation of Asian tigers, the beauty of wildlife, and the importance of forests. In it, a ghost tiger sends a message to the living tigers, telling them how to escape poachers and survive the changes happening to the forest.

How many times have you worn your tiger costume and performed the piece? So many times I've lost count! Our company has given many performances in Malaysia, but we've also traveled abroad to conferences such as the United Nations Environment Programme. In 2011, we performed "The Phantom Tiger" in Washington, D.C., for the World Children's Festival.

JES ISMAEL IZAIDIN

I FILED A LAWSUIT AGAINST THE UNITED STATES OF AMERICA.

ALEC LOORZ, 16 YEARS OLD IN 2011, VENTURA, CALIFORNIA, UNITED STATES

BACKGROUND

The climate of our planet is warming. The consequence is that glaciers are melting and the oceans are expanding, raising the level of the sea.

For Alec, if global warming is a reality today, it's because the United States didn't do enough in the past to protect the Earth for future generations. He believes that the government has relied on money from fossil fuel companies to remain inactive on the subject of climate change, and that the government hasn't accepted its responsibilities to take action and address the climate problem.

Alec decided he had to do something to get the leaders of the United States to pay attention. Along with others, he filed a lawsuit against the federal government of the United States for not acting responsibly. His actions prompted other young people to do the same in all fifty states. If Alec wins his suit, the government must immediately repair the damage done to the environment.

Storm over the Loita Hills in Kenya.

"IN THE EARLY YEARS OF MY CAMPAIGN, I WANTED TO ASK THE COURT IF JUSTICE WOULD BE SERVED, AND WE WOULD SEE REAL CHANGE."

ALEC LOORZ

ALEC LOORZ

Alec has been fighting against climate change since he saw the film *An Inconvenient Truth* when he was twelve. Afterward, he began a tour to schools to explain to students about climate change. He then founded the organization "Kids vs. Global Warming."

Alec has organized youth marches called the iMatter March, in 200 countries with the message: "Our Future Matters!"

www.imattermarch.org
www.kids-vs-global-warming.com/Home.html

OBJECTIVE: Fight against global warming and climate change.

ACTION: File a lawsuit against the United States government.

HOW I'VE CHANGED THE WORLD: More than 300,000 people, especially young people, are aware of global warming because of my presentations. We conducted peaceful protest marches around the world including the United States, India, Pakistan, and Sierra Leone.

WHAT I'M MOST PROUD OF: The "iMatter" marches. It was great to receive pictures from the protests that took place all over the world. My association launched the idea, and the countries organized the marches after that.

MY MOST HEROIC ACTION: I gave a speech on the subject of climate change to a school where students said that I had come to present propaganda. But I went ahead with the speech, and when I was done, 500 of the 750 students decided to commit that day to act against climate change.

MY BIGGEST MISTAKE: The truth is, it's a fault of mine. I've met a number of extraordinary people and I've failed to keep in touch with them. I regret it and I'm trying to improve.

HOW DO MY PARENTS SUPPORT ME: My mom works full-time for Kids vs. Global Warming.

MY ADVICE: Everyone must find a mission. There are opportunities out there that you could never have imagined.

WHAT I DO NOW: We still do great iMatter events. I'm continuing to talk with young activists who want to see change in our world.

ALEX LOORZ

123

GETTING INVOLVED

● ● ● ● ● ● ● ● ● ● ● ● ● ● ● ● ● ● ● ●

The kids you've read about in this book come from many different countries, focus on many different causes, and have taken many different approaches to effecting change. But if there's one thing they have in common, it's *passion* for taking a stand and making a difference. One of the kids in this book even has some advice on this front: As Alex Lin says, "Find something that excites you, and do it. If you're not passionate about something, it's harder to stay motivated when things get complicated." It seems like passion is a majorly important part of what helps kids make a difference. So to help you figure out how to take action, let's think about what *you're* passionate about!

There are tons of different organizations out there dedicated to making a better world—so many that it can be a little overwhelming. In order to figure out what organization is the best fit for you, we've categorized them by subject matter, and even provided a description of what kind of work each one does. The organizations included range from world-wide societies to the groups started by the kids featured in this book. So read on, and discover how to use your passion to become a kid who changes the world!

WORKING WITH THE ENVIRONMENT

If you're passionate about the physical world around you, then keep reading! When it comes to the environment, there are lots of different ways you can help. Some people focus on preserving wildlife, while others try to prevent the growing problem of global warming. Look through the organizations listed below to find out which one fits you the best.

• • • • • • • • • • • • • • • • • • • •

WILDLIFE CONSERVATION

OCEANA

Oceana was founded in 2001 and remains the largest international organization focused on ocean conservation. They see the importance of identifying scientific problems and finding solutions that can be done by their offices all over the world. By working with economists, lawyers, and advocates, Oceana hopes to revive the ocean. They are focused on crises such as overfishing, acidification, and habitat destruction. You can find lots of ways to help on their website, including becoming a Wavemaker or attending one of their events.

➤ Visit them at: oceana.org

NATIONAL FISH AND WILDLIFE CONSERVATION

Congress created the NFWF in 1984, and since then they have worked with both the public and private sectors to protect our nation's fish, wildlife, plants, and habitats. NFWF brings everyone together to stress the importance of our habitats, promote healthy oceans, and conserve water for wildlife and people. You can see their long list of conservation programs on their website.

➤ Visit them at: nfwf.org

THE ENDANGERED SPECIES PROGRAM

It's important to protect all the animals on our planet, especially endangered species. The U.S. Fish and Wildlife Service aims to protect endangered and threatened species, and conserve species that could become threatened. They work to protect animals of all kinds and partner with landowners and tribes to save these animals. You can learn more about protecting nature at their website, where they also have lot of great information for research projects and reports.

➤ Visit them at: fws.gov/letsgooutside

THE NATIONAL WILDLIFE FEDERATION

People have become disconnected with nature, a fact that the National Wildlife Federation is trying to change. They are working on protecting the ecosystems that are crucial to wildlife. Another way they've improved wildlife conservation is by changing policies that affect public, private, and tribal lands. They hope this in turn will benefit humanity as a whole. NWF's "BE OUT THERE" campaign wants to push you away from the TV and into nature. You can play games and learn fun facts on their website.

➤ Visit them at: nwf.org/kids.aspx

WORLD WILDLIFE FUND

WWF works in 100 countries and is supported by 5 million members globally, which helps them meet the needs of both people and nature. They work to conserve nature and save the planet, with the help of individuals and groups around the world. You can participate in Earth Hour, travel with WWF, or even adopt an animal!

➤ Visit them at: gowild.wwf.org.uk

DEFENDERS OF WILDLIFE

Defenders of Wildlife works to conserve wildlife and the natural habitats they live in. They want North America's animals to stay as strong, beautiful, and plentiful as possible for future generations. They release animals into their natural habitat, rally about policy change, and most importantly, bring awareness to the dangers these animals face. You can get involved by adopting an animal or becoming a Wildlife Guardian.

➤ Visit them at: defenders.org/mission-and-vision

PETA KIDS

People for the Ethical Treatment of Animals (PETA) has over 2 million members, making them the largest animal rights organization in the world. They know animals should have basic rights, just like we do. PETA works to make sure animals are treated well in places like farms, laboratories, and on sets of movies and TV shows. They do this by educating the public, doing research and investigations, and rescuing animals.

➤ Visit them at: petakids.com

GREENPEACE

Greenpeace wants to protect the planet in the most direct way possible. They investigate and confront environmental abuse and urge people to be environmentally responsible with their actions. You can sign up and see events and get resources. You can volunteer, or even take action now by using your voice against upcoming policies.

➤ Visit them at: greenpeace.org/usa/en

SIERRA CLUB

"Explore, Enjoy and Protect the Planet" is the Sierra Club's motto. The Sierra Club made strides in protecting the environment, such as helping pass the Clean Water Act, Clean Air Act, and the Endangered Species Act. Lately they've been working on moving away from using fossil fuels, and moving the country towards a clean energy economy. You can volunteer during one of the many outings they have every year, or become a leader in your community by visiting their ClubHub page.

➤ Visit them at: sierraclub.org

WILDLIFE CONSERVATION SOCIETY

Founded in 1895, the Wildlife Conservation Society strives to save wildlife and wild places all around the world. They manage more than 200 million acres of protected land and work with more than 200 scientists. Working with the New York City parks, they have created the world's most comprehensive conservation organization. All 5 parks help educate millions of people each year in science and conservation issues. In addition, they have a Family Fun Run every year in support of an animal in need of help.

➤ Visit them at: wcs.org

JOIN IN WITH KIDS WHO HAVE HELPED CONSERVE WILDLIFE:

CAMERON OLIVER

page 16

Cameron discovered that 1 in 2 camels die from eating litter left in the desert by humans, and decided to do something about it. Here, you can catch up with Cameron's campaign and learn some facts. You can also learn how to prevent this unnecessary littering and save the camels.

➤ Visit Cameron's website at: cameronscamelcampaign.com

OLIVIA BOULER

page 36

Olivia has been able to raise over $200,000 to help save birds suffering from the oil spill in the gulf. You can help too! By going to her website, you can learn more about what she's been up to and can even buy her book "Olivia's Birds: Saving the Gulf."

➤ Visit Olivia's website at: oliviabouler.net

JAMES BROOKS

page 98

When James Brooks learned that the great apes of the Congo were disappearing, he knew he needed to take action. Through his research, he learned that the people of the Congo were struggling too. He decided to help both animals and people by providing information on the endangered apes through ApeAware, and working with the 1000 Classrooms project to help raise awareness about, and improve, the situation in the

Democratic Republic of Congo. You can help save apes and people by checking out their website.

➤ Visit James's website at: apeaware.org
➤ Join the 1000 Classrooms project at: 1000classrooms.org

ONDINE ELIOT

page 110

Ondine knows that even though sharks have a bad reputation, they need our help as much as any other animal. We have to work together to make sure they don't go extinct. Her blog explains some of the injustices sharks face, and why we should save them.

➤ Visit Ondine's website at: passiondesrequins.skyrock.com

JES ISMAEL IZAIDIN

page 118

There are tons of ways to bring attention to a problem, and one of those is art. Jes took his love of art and used it to communicate the suffering of Asian Tigers, and why we need to help them. You can find out more about his current efforts at his website.

➤ Visit Jes's website at: treetg.com/aboutus.html

CLIMATE CHANGE

TREE PEOPLE

Cities contribute 80 percent of greenhouse gas emissions, which is a cause of global warming. TreePeople understands the importance of improving the environment on a local level. They are helping create a sustainable future for Los Angeles, California. Planting more trees can help create cooler temperatures, cleaner air, and replenished groundwater supplies. You can learn how to plant and care for a tree, along with lots of other helpful info, at their website.

➤ Visit them at: treepeople.org/who-we-are

THE GREEN SQUAD

The Natural Resource Defense Council works to safeguard the earth, including its people, animals, plants, and natural systems. You can be a part of their Greensquad. This is an awesome website where you can learn how to change the world around you, just by changing things in your classroom. Then you can share this with your friends and teachers, and they can be your Greensquad Team!

➤ Visit them at: nrdc.org/greensquad

KIDS F.A.C.E

Kids F.A.C.E (Kids For A Clean Environment) knows even one person can help change the world. They started as a small group with only 6 members, but they now have over

300,000 and have planted over 1 million trees. Membership is free and you can join them in saving the planet.

➤ Visit them at: kidsface.org/pages/thefacts.html

ROOTS AND SHOOTS

Created by Dr. Jane Goodall, Roots and Shoots aims to make positive things happen. They connect youth of all ages across 120 countries, who want to help make the world a better place to live now, and in the future. We can identify problems in our area and start service-projects to create solutions. Check out their website to find project ideas, get inspired, and discover project toolkits!

➤ Visit them at: rootsandshoots.org

JOIN IN WITH KIDS WHO HAVE WORKED WITH CLIMATE CHANGE:

AITAN GROSSMAN

page 18

Global warming is a very real problem that is only getting worse. Aitan is asking for help. He created a "100 generations" song, and you can sing it with him on his website. If you buy a copy of the song, money will be donated to environmental groups that are working to stop climate change.

Visit Aitan's website at: kidearth.us

PARKER LIAUTAUD

page 76

Parker needs everyone to know how dangerous climate change can be. On his trips to Antarctica, he could see physical changes from climate change, and now he wants to share that with the world. Find out more at his website and learn about his expeditions!

➤ Visit Parker's website at: parkerliautaud.com

ALEC LOORZ

page 120

Alec felt like the government wasn't doing enough to address the issue of global warming, so he decided to do something about it. He believes the government can help save the environment, but we need to show them how. The iMatter Marches around the world are one way to raise awareness, but you can also check out Alec's website for a bunch of other resources.

➤ Visit Alec's website at: kids-vs-global-warming.com/Home.html
➤ Visit the iMatter March website at: imattermarch.org

ANUP RAJ CHALISE

page 28

As trees grow, they absorb gasses in the atmosphere. This helps manage global warming. Anup was able to persuade his community to plant pipals, which was not only environmentally beneficial but supported their religious practices. You can learn more at his website, and see pictures of all the work being done in Nepal.

➤ Visit Anup's website at: ficusreligiosaanup.yolasite.com

ADELINE SUWANA

page 80

Adeline created Sahabat Alam to teach people about the environment, and to encourage people of any age to get involved with nature. Visit the Sahabat Alam website to see how you can help, and how you can teach your friends about protecting nature around you.

➤ Visit Adeline's website at: sahabat-alam.com/en/

FELIX FINKBEINER

page 90

When Felix learned that trees help reduce global warming, he decided to create an organization that would get kids around the world planting trees to help combat the effects of climate change. Plant-for-the-Planet is taking a stand and fighting against the injustices being done to the earth. Visit their website to find tons of cool information and learn some ways you can help.

➤ Visit Felix's website at: plant-for-the-planet.org/en/

HELPING PEOPLE AROUND THE WORLD

If you're passionate about helping people, whether it's someone across the world or right in your backyard, this is the section for you. Problems like poverty and hunger exist in countries all over the world. Keep reading to find out how you can help combat these issues.

• •

HEIFER INTERNATIONAL

Heifer International works with communities to end world hunger and poverty, while still taking care of the Earth. They aim to change hunger and poverty into hope and prosperity. The goal is not just to provide temporary relief, but to create a solution that allows communities to care and provide for themselves in a sustainable way.

➤ Visit them at: heifer.org/about-heifer/index.html

FREE THE CHILDREN

Children are our future, and no one knows that more than Free the Children. They are a charity that pushes children all over the world to reach their potential. By doing this, children can make a difference in their community and become active global citizens. They encourage us to think about what we do and the way we do it to make a bigger and better impact on the world. You can find out how you can get involved by checking out their website.

➤ Visit them at: freethechildren.com

UNICEF

The United Nations Children's Fund (UNICEF) provides health care, clean water, sanitation, nutrition, education, and emergency relief to children all over the world. Their goal is to improve children's lives everywhere and to live in a world where zero children die of things we can prevent. See the many ways to join UNICEF's team on their website.

➤ Visit them at: unicefusa.org

WORLD FOOD PROGRAMME

The World Food Programme is the world's largest humanitarian agency fighting hunger worldwide. Their important work includes getting food to necessary areas, saving the lives of victims of war, and using food to help communities rebuild after a crisis. They want every man, woman, and child to lead an active and healthy life. Their goal is to help people around the world so that organizations like theirs are no longer needed. You can learn more about them, and even play their FreeRice game at this site!

➤ Visit them at: wfp.org

FEEDING AMERICA

Feeding America urges us to remember that hunger is also a large problem in developed countries like America. With the help of food banks and communities, they have been able to educate officials and feed those in need. But the battle isn't over yet; millions of Americans are still in need of a sufficient food source. Visit their website to discover interesting facts, read inspiring stories, and find a way to take action.

➤ Visit them at: feedingamerica.org

CONVOY OF HOPE

Convoy of Hope tries to bring help and hope to those who are impoverished, hungry, and hurting. They engage communities by holding events with free goods and services, partnering with churches to provide mentoring and training, and serving meals to hundreds of thousands of children. They also help people learn to farm, and respond to disasters around the world. You can help by volunteering, attending events, or holding fund-raisers.

➤ Visit them at: convoyofhope.org

MERCYCORPS

MercyCorps works in some of the world's toughest places, such as failing states or conflict zones, where they help make sure families are safe, educated, and equipped to provide for themselves. They know strong and safe communities are the best way to reach success. You can attend events or partner with them to directly impact and improve lives.

➤ Visit them at: mercycorps.org

OXFAM INTERNATIONAL

One out of three people in the world is living in poverty. Oxfam works to help families climb their way to a better quality of life, and thrive. They also want those people to have a say in the policies and global decisions that affect them. As they educate and help these people in need, they are creating a stronger tomorrow. You can work with them or follow their accomplishments on their website.

➤ Visit them at: oxfam.org/en

WORLD VISION INTERNATIONAL

World Vision International works to make their vision of a better world come true. They strive to help all children grow up healthy, strong, protected, and with opportunity. They focus on ending poverty by allowing communities to take charge of their futures. Ten million supporters are committed to making these changes in the world, and you can be too!

➤ Visit them at: wvi.org

JOIN IN WITH KIDS WHO HAVE WORKED TO HELP PEOPLE ALL OVER THE WORLD:

TA'KAIYA BLANEY

page 52

Ta'Kaiya has been trying to educate people everywhere about the dangers of the Northern Gateway Pipeline, and the threat it poses to the culture of the First Nations territories. She knows the environment and its people are important. You can see her work, and her video "Shallow Water" on her website, along with her other music and art.

➤ Visit Ta'Kaiya's website at: takaiyablaney.com

RUJUL ZAPARDE

page 64

When Rujul visited relatives in Paras, India, he couldn't believe that not everyone had drinking water. He knew he had to find a way to help Paras, so he started an organization with his friends to raise money for well construction.

1

Drinking Water for India has built 56 wells in India, and continues to help people access fresh water. Everyone should be able to drink clean water, and you can help make this a reality. Check out the website to learn more about the cause, and how to get your school involved.

➤ Visit Rujul's website at: drinkingwaterforindia.org